Batch

Craft, Design and Product

Batch

Craft, Design and Product

LEARNING
RESOURCES
CENTRE
HAVERING
COLLEGE

Andrew Tanner

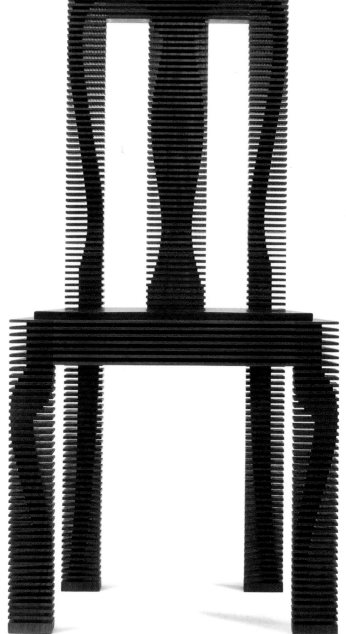

A&
CB

Contents

First published in Great Britain 2010
A & C Black Publishers Limited
36 Soho Square
London W1D 3QY
www.acblack.com

ISBN 978-1-4081-1008-9

CIP Catalogue records for this
book are available from the
British Library.

Book design by Elizabeth Healey
Cover design by Sutchinda Thompson

Printed and bound in China.

This book is produced using paper
that is made from wood grown in
managed, sustainable forests. It is
natural, renewable and recyclable. The
logging and manufacturing processes
conform to the environmental regulations of the country of origin.

Images
Title page: Flames by Chris Kabel, powder
coated gas pipes and fittings, gas cartridge
holder, 2003. Photo courtesy of the artist.
Anne Chair by Gareth Neal, American walnut,
2009. Photo by Ian Forsyth.
Frontispiece: Hooks and Frocks by Deb
Bowness, digital and silkscreen printing on
wallpaper, 1999. Photo courtesy of the artist.

Acknowledgements

Thanks to the organisations who support craft and design and encourage the next generation of designers, makers and craftspeople to nurture their creative attributes and endorse their journeys through design. To the consumer who takes time to look underneath products to read the back-stamp and see who the designer is behind the object, the story and the origin of manufacture and who buy objects with distinction, originality and craftsmanship. Thanks to the 50 plus designers, makers, craftspeople and industry leaders who have contributed their time and honesty through interviews for this book, many of whom are dear friends and make trade fairs less painful; and to the late Peta Levi MBE, to whom I and many others owe gratitude for her relentless support and passion through design.

Thanks to Suzanne, Darcie and Florence, to whom I owe the countless days of sledging and playing in the sun that I missed whilst compiling and researching the book. Thanks also to Emma, Barry, Stephen, Angel and Claire, and to Anna and Jim with whom I started the journey in design over a decade ago and still look back with admiration for our determination.

Finally, to my mother, father and sister who have been, and continue to be, pillars of support throughout my career.

Disclaimer

The views and opinions expressed in this book do not necessarily represent the views of Andrew Tanner or A & C Black. No responsibility for loss occasioned to any person by acting or refraining from action in reliance on the book, its contributors or author can be accepted by the contributors of this publication.

Left
TITLE: Oriental Tub Chair
ARTIST: Helen Amy Murray
MATERIAL: 'Cool black' leather and reflective fabric
PHOTO: Marcos Bevilacqua

Preface

Whether looking to commission design, buy design, create design or simply like immersing yourself into the world of design, *Batch* will introduce you to a behind the scenes, open studio tour of some of the most recognised movers and shakers the craft, product and design world has to offer. Each entry details a designer's journey from glassware and its blowers, ceramicists and their throwing to surface designers and their inspiration. And for when you want to leave the comfort of your home, we have compiled a guide to the best places to view work online or buy it on the high street.

The world of the designer-maker is open for business and, with that in mind, one of the aims of this book is to encourage the next generation of designers into joining the creative community with some of the essentials that university may never have prepared for. We ask the designers for their advice on setting up a studio, the importance of understanding a market place and why a unique selling point is fundamental in

creating your own story behind a product. *Batch* brings you interviews with established makers and emerging designers, conversations with a journalist, an exhibition curator, a retailer and even an accountant. Their observations strips bare the real world of the maker, designer and craftsman offering advice from the other side of the fence and an end consumer perspective.

Craftsmanship, products and the importance of design are radically being brought together as we begin to detox our homes and interiors from mass produced cloned product and revert to the values of investing in a conversation piece and objects which reflect our individual personalities. Just as every picture tells a story, so every piece of craft conveys a journey undertaken.

Batch aims to not only tell these stories but inspire others to follow in the footsteps of those featured in the book, whether through joining evening classes and university courses, partaking in craft and trade fairs or investing in original craft, design or product.

Introduction

Today's generation of makers are fluent in product design, have a knowledge of more than just one material, but most importantly are building bridges between fashion, lifestyle, media and craft.

Playing and empathising with materials is fundamental to creating craft. It's about being hands on, getting your hands messy, and bringing together old techniques with new processes whilst pushing the boundaries to create unique outcomes.

In the 1990s our homes became awash with cloned product design purchased through large retailers creating high-volume, low-profit manufactured items. This book has been written as a celebration of the work of designers and makers who are challenging this established mass-market manufacture with the production of craft-based items.

Many of the designers selected for the book make the work themselves in small batches or as one-offs using the same processes. Others work with traditional manufacturers and challenge our industrial heritage with new takes on old processes. Some bridge advances in technology with craft and product whilst others are an industry of one, themselves being the production line, the manufacturer, the designer and the maker.

Stereotypes play a crucial part in the refining of the word 'craft'. Bearded potters and their wheels conjure up medieval undertones that today's craftsmen and women are challenging by bringing craft and design to a closer proximity than ever before.

Capturing this transformation in craft and design pivots around the debate of 'What's in a name'? Words or terms can lean toward stereotypes and can limit our ability to progress and develop by way of new materials, mediums and outcomes. Any attempt to respond to the question 'What do you call yourself?' can restrict the designer and crafts-maker to the constraints of a title rather than expanding their horizons through the pursuit of a process or in reaction to a problem which needs solving. How someone defines their 'title' is therefore crucial to how they wish themselves and their work to be seen. Just as the word 'contemporary' has been overused and deserves to have its own Trade Descriptions Act associated with it, so too have the words 'designer', 'craftsperson' and 'artisan'. In the rise of home improvement television in the mid 1990's the title of 'Interior Designer' became mainstream and anyone with a paintbrush and a Dulux colour card seemed to use it.

The rise of a creative nation should be applauded, however. How do we distinguish between followers and leaders of fashion? How can we define craft as being, well, craft?

Opposite

TITLE: '8.5' Glazed Porcelain

ARTIST: KleinReid

MATERIAL: Porcelain with
Curry Yellow glaze,
developed in the studio

DATE: 2009

PHOTO: KleinReid

Left

TITLE: Wasso

ARTIST: Tait and Style

MATERIAL: 100% Wool

DATE: 2005

PHOTO: John Paul

Below

TITLE: Jigsaw
ARTIST: Tracey Kendall
MATERIAL: Non-woven
wallpaper, screenprinted
with reclaimed cardboard
jigsaw
DATE: 2005
PHOTO: Rachel Smith/
c/o artist

The answer lies behind our empathy and recognition towards the amount of work employed behind a product or piece of work. Whether it be in recognition for hours of labour, the amount of blisters one has on their hands, the years of education, time taken to solve a problem or in the craft and skill passed down from generation to generation from dove tail joints to copper wheel engraving. It is the story and journey behind the product we use to justify 'craft'.

Hundreds of craft fairs across the world attract buyers wanting something unique and bespoke. There is still a traditional ground for exhibiting craft, but they are radically changing, as is the work of the craftsperson. The word 'craft' has perhaps become dated over the past decade. With the creative community developing and diversifying, so have the craftsmen and women. In the early 1990s the Schools of Art and universities gave birth to what was perceived as the answer; 'the designer-maker'. Taking craft and crossbreeding it with the cool world of design created a new hybrid title that was as ambiguous and diverse as the work the designer-maker created. Thus it placed the craftsperson into a marketplace to which trend forecasters, interior stylists and lifestyle editors turned to source the latest in design.

The maker becomes a visionary who creates movements for others to follow. Knitting and knitted objects have become much sought-after thanks to makers such as Donna Wilson and her knitted doughnuts which in turn invite a DIY nation to try their hand and before you know it, sewing is fashionable again with Stitch groups and Knit groups happening across the country over a glass of wine. Even the WI has been revamped with an Institute opening at Goldsmiths University in London with creativity no doubt at the top of the activity list.

Craft not only responds to our industrial heritage and historic foundations but evidently sets pace for new material experimentations. Playing and empathising with materials is fundamental to creating craft. It's about being hands on, getting your hands messy, and bringing together old techniques with new processes whilst pushing the boundaries to create unique outcomes. In 2010 the prestigious UK based Crafts Council Craft Fair titled 'Origin' moves to a new venue to become part of the London Design festival underlining the importance of synergy and energy between craft and design.

The crafts person is not shy to collaborate and network, mix and share knowledge in moving their practices forward. Ceramicists are working with textile makers and furniture designers are collaborating with glass manufacturers in the creation of new outcomes and new marriages in design.

Whoever we are and whatever we call ourselves we are blurring the boundaries between traditional craft and contemporary design.

The 1990s reflected a significant move in art colleges and universities. Artists such as Damien Hirst and Tracey Emin were taking part in Sensation, the notorious exhibition at the Royal Academy in 1997, and graduates from craft-skilled courses began to create outcomes which pushed craft into a design arena. Exhibitions such as New Designers; an annual launchpad for graduate design which is based at the Business Design Centre, London, offered a platform for recent graduates to show their work and find buyers. However, these buyers were also changing. Fashion retailers began to sell product close to the haute-couture fashion world of bespoke, small-scale, limited-edition, hand-produced, batch-produced craft.

Today's generation of makers are fluent in product design, having a knowledge of more than just one material, but most importantly they are building bridges between fashion, lifestyle, media and craft. The only problem is that our university courses, unlike the designers which emerge from them, have not kept up with the times and are inade-quately prepared to support students with life after graduation.

Change is happening, however, with some universities finally realising that a degree show to which you can invite your family at the end of three years may not be enough to kick-start a career in the design world.

With additional schemes such as the Crafts Council's Next Move, and new marriages being created between education providers and entrepreneurs, slowly a new support system is being built

Right
TITLE: Ladder Bookcase
ARTIST: Autoban
MATERIAL: Wood
DATE: 2006
PHOTO: Autoban/De La Espada

to encourage the future creative community who can make a difference to our visual environment.

Just as the craft and design world move closer together, as too does the manufacture and production of craft and design. In the UK our industrial heritage prided itself on bringing craft to a larger market through Stoke-on-Trent Ceramics (in use by the likes of myself, Scabetti and Kathleen Hills) and the Yorkshire textile Mills (Margo Selby).

It appears that finally, traditional manufacturing houses are being exposed to the consumer, their geographic location and ethical working practice playing an important part in the final make-up of a product. Through this explosion of manufacturing possibilities, the maker is able to research manufacturing over the internet and find ethical, traditional and sustainable processes of manufacture to make their work in the same way as they would have done if making just a single item. As the world's marketplace for craft and manufacture unites a new marriage between craft, design and manufacture is being created.

The unsung heroes of the manufacturing world who have traditionally concentrated on producing their own work are now more open to collaborating with and naming other designers. The personalisation of a product is important to the consumer; we like to see a name behind the design, allowing us to build a relationship between the product and the person who made or designed the piece. Retailers such as John Lewis Partnerships in the UK have started to name the designers behind the product and people are once again picking up objects to read the backstamp.

Within the vast brick walls of industry there are skilled people with an unprecedented knowledge of traditional production processes, offering the consumer an affordable product with an identifiable maker.

A support system connecting the industrial heritage of the UK to designers is a long way off but the challenge is being met head on by the crafts people themselves to form manufacturing marriages, knocking on the doors of manufacture and formulating ways of working. Heritage plays an important role to Craft and Design and I only hope that someone realises this before it's not too late. I was once told by my manufacturer that it is easy to close a factory, but a lot harder to reopen one.

Above

TITLE: Fairpom Cushions
ARTIST: Tait and Style
MATERIAL: Fairisle knitting combined with woven lambswool
DATE: 1992
PHOTO: Gunnie Moberg

Centre

TITLE: Fisheye Plate
ARTIST: Stuart Akroyd
MATERIAL: Twice-blown glass
DATE: 2007
PHOTO: Tim Spriddell

Right

TITLE: People Bookmark
ARTIST: Rebecca Joselyn
MATERIAL: Silver
DATE: 2008
PHOTO: Jerry Lampson

Whether a craftsperson decides to collaborate with industry on this scale is not important. What is important, though, is that the maker is able to produce work which can be bought by greater numbers of people through an increased number of outlets. Achieving a price point lower than a maker could achieve when making the work themselves, but retaining the thought and quality behind the work, propels the maker into a new arena of retail outlets, design boutiques and even chain stores.

This book promotes a portfolio of those makers who have pushed boundaries and different processes, and in doing so have become leaders of their profession. In addition the book introduces the new emerging talent of those who will carve our futures through craft, design and product.

Showcasing work by material and discipline, seven chapters are dedicated to the work of the makers. Each artist has a different story to tell within the context of their practice from the areas of ceramics, furniture, metal and jewellery, glass, textiles, multi-disciplinary design and wall-surface design and decoration.

The final chapter, called Behind the Scenes, is comprised of a series of interviews with various prime movers in the design world, not designers themselves, but experts in their field. These people are hugely influential and knowledgeable in how to go about joining the ranks of esteemed, successful designer-makers such as those featured in this book, whilst encouraging newcomers to become part of this evolving creative community.

Craft not only responds to our industrial heritage and historic foundations but evidently sets pace for new material experimentations. Playing and empathising with materials is fundamental to creating craft. It's about being hands on, getting your hands messy, and bringing together old techniques with new processes whilst pushing the boundaries to create unique outcomes.

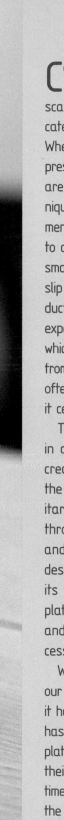

Ceramics

Ceramics and its production methods lend themselves beautifully to the craft of small-scale production. Ceramic production falls into two categories: either 'one-off' or 'batch-produced'. Whether the ceramics are thrown, slipcast, press-moulded or handbuilt, designers and makers are beginning to explore these traditional techniques and bring them into contemporary environments. The maker has at their disposal the ability to create a batch production line of work within a small space requiring access to just plaster, clay, slip and kiln. It is this accessibility for batch production which tempts many young designers into experimenting with ceramic objects. Today, forms which would normally be disposed of are being cast from everyday objects and given a new lease of life, often prompting the question from the consumer 'Is it ceramic?'.

This section offers designers who have trained in and continue to experiment with ceramics to create products which push the boundaries of the material. Lighting, wall art and everyday utilitarian products encapsulate traditional values through contemporary design. It is not just form and shape which are being addressed by the designer; surface pattern and design is making its way from the constraints of paper onto the plate. Graphic designers, textile designers, artists and illustrators are bringing 2D into 3D with accessories for the home and interiors.

With manufacturing increasing in the Far East our industrial heritage is under the greatest threat it has faced for many years. However, the market has reached saturation point, with white porcelain plates and mugs selling at prices not dissimilar to their cardboard throwaway counterparts. So, its time to lift up those plates when shopping and read the back stamp, be different from the Joneses and buy products with individuality and character.

Opposite
TITLE: Crate
ARTIST: Hub (see Andrew Tanner)
MATERIAL: Slipcast earthenware ceramic with white glaze
DATE: 1999
PHOTO: Sally Bream

Hub had three fantastic years in which we saw our company go from strength to strength. We designed under our own copyright to our own project briefs and made everything ourselves.

When I was growing up, my family used to go on holiday to Poole in Dorset in England. I recall visiting Poole Pottery, where at the entrance to the factory shop was a water fountain made from thirty or so of their iconic ceramic dolphins. I would return year after year with my parents, who were and still are avid collectors of ceramics.

In 1997 I graduated from the University of Brighton, where I studied wood, metal, ceramics and plastics. The course introduced me to slipcasting and small-scale batch production. Most importantly, it introduced me to ways of transferring textures from an original source to another surface.

I was excited by the notion that replicated textures and forms could then be transformed to create new outcomes. By changing the material of a disposable object but keeping the form, you increase the lifespan of that form, which would otherwise be discarded after use.

After leaving university it soon became apparent that I had to create a workplace for myself, as finding one would be almost impossible. Like many others, I exhibited at the New Designers exhibition in London. This was when I realised how competitive the design marketplace was and continues to be. I took with me two products, one, entitled 'padded cell', a design for a floor tile inspired by the soft cushioning on a Mies van der Rohe day chair, and the other a range of earthenware slipcast ceramic sculptures. The ceramic sculpture received little interest, but the tiles, because there was a function attached to the concept, began to draw in visitors at the show, in particular press and PR.

In October 1997 the interiors and style magazine *Wallpaper* published their round-up of who they deemed to be the designers of the future. 'They're young, hip, fresh out of college and this

won't be the last you hear of them' read the article, which included, along with five other designers, myself, Bodo Sperlein and Anna Thomson, who would become my business partner for the next three years.

I had no money and had to go searching for funding to start up in business. Having enjoyed similar successful experiences with our work at the New Designers exhibition, Anna Thomson and I decided to apply to the Prince's Youth Business Trust, who awarded us a £5000 loan, and in December 1998 we formed a ceramic design company called Hub, which stood for the 'centre of activity'.

Hub had three fantastic years in which we saw our company go from strength to strength. We designed under our own copyright to our own project briefs and made everything ourselves. Slipcasting and glazing work were done in an old warehouse in Brighton. We designed a number of

products, some of which I still have in my portfolio today. The first product for which we needed to find a manufacturer was the Crate Fruit Holder (see p.14). Designed in 1998, the product was soon selling in numbers far greater than we could keep up with, so after going through the Yellow Pages we set out in our car to Stoke-on-Trent to find suitable manufacturers.

In 2001, Hub was awarded the Crafts Council Development Grant, and we had managed to collect a number of awards whilst selling to retailers we could have only dreamed about reaching – Harrods in London, Donna Karan in New York, and Barneys Japan – together with over fifty independent design boutiques in Britain and other countries.

In December 2002 we decided to go our separate ways. Anna and I still work together on a number of different projects, but as a design partnership we were finding it difficult financially

to feed two mouths. In February of that year I started Andrew Tanner Design.

The collection Flock, which was designed toward the end of the Hub period, won best new product in 2001. I was unaware that I was ahead of my time in drawing inspiration from wallpaper, that the press exposure this collection obtained would help carve a trend for wallpaper, yet now there is not a DIY chain on the high street which does not sell baroque-print and flock-effect wall coverings.

My first collaboration was with the wonderful wallpaper company Cole and Son, who are visionaries in their field. They asked if I would produce a collection of ceramics inspired by their archive, and I was so taken with this idea that drawing information from the past to create new outcomes in design has been my inspiration ever since.

I see the past as a kind of hidden treasure chest, and I am passionate about traditional manufacturing that can still be useful in the modern world. Likewise with surface pattern and decoration, the past holds the answer to future trends and offers a great starting point for seeing how far concepts can be pushed without losing the original story.

In 2005 IPC media announced that I had won Young Designer of the Year and also that I had won my client Maw and Company, a traditional tile company based in the heart of Stoke-on-Trent,

Above

TITLE: Flocked, flying bird
MATERIAL: Earthenware, black glaze
DATE: 2007
PHOTO: El Managerio

Below

TITLE: Silhouette Wall Plate (detail)
MATERIAL: Bone china, pierced design
DATE: 2006
PHOTO: El Managerio

the award for best surface design. The attention I got from the award propelled me into creating further collections for bespoke clients.

The Crafts Council, the Arts Council and the Department of Trade and Investment have all given financial backing to my projects as well as an education in business matters. In 2008 I applied to the Arts Council to support a major project of mine to design a range of products which would celebrate British design and manufacture. Inspired by the lack of story-based product and relevant souvenirs available at British tourist sites, especially as we prepare for the global platform provided by the 2012 Olympics in London, the project has created new marriages and new collections which will be sold through UK tourist attractions. After all, there is a limit to how many pencils and rubbers, jams and pickles you feel you need after visiting one of these places of interest.

Today my personal journey continues as I work with one of the British gems of the ceramic industry and find myself at the point where I began. As Head of Design for Poole Pottery and Royal Stafford, I find myself let loose in a sweet shop of historical treasures and personal memories, but with a challenging brief: to create new outcomes through traditional manufacture for the next generation of buyers.

This book has been produced to encourage new designers. My advice is to listen to each of the designers and makers in this book so that you may draw your own conclusions. Learning by your mistakes is a good philosophy, but given a little help from your peers it may not always be necessary. Finally, remember to pass on the baton of knowledge that's been handed to you.

Above

TITLE: The Art of
Entertaining, British
Creamware collection
DATE: 2009
PHOTO: Kill the Film

Right

TITLE: Heritage Wall
Vase, Souvenirs Worth
Giving collection
DATE: 2010
PHOTO: Kill the Film

Cobwebs, branches, berries and surface patterns resembling droplets of rain all delicately spread themselves across the forms of beautiful white bone-china tableware forms and accessories.

The Oxo Tower in London is home to over 25 design practices, including the studio of Bodo Sperlein. The interior is cleverly divided with a retail counter, a small but perfectly proportioned retail space and, behind what can only be described as a hidden wall concealed by wood panelling, Bodo's personal design space. In the latter, floor-to-ceiling shelves hold inspirational books and back catalogues of his press exposure since his launch in 1997 at the New Designers exhibition in London.

Bodo Sperlein is a well-recognised and important designer successfully representing British design and manufacture. Although his signature collections are predominantly in ceramics, he works across a selection of other materials. Bodo also works as a design consultant for a range of different clients.

Born in Germany, Bodo came to the UK and embarked on a career very different to what he is doing today. Whilst searching for decorative accessories to fill his home in London, he realised that it was difficult to find design-led ceramics that could be both decorative and functional. He enrolled on an afternoon course in ceramics, where, surrounded by other practising recreational artisans, he found release from his job as a marketing consultant and bilingual translator. Two years on and by continuing his passion for ceramics through part-time education, he finally applied for a place at Camberwell College of Arts and studied for his BA

Above right
TITLE: Re-Cyclos Magical Collection by Bodo Sperlein for Lladro.
MATERIAL: Gres black porcelain
DATE: 2007
PHOTO: Rachael Smith

Right
TITLE: Black Forest Décor for Dibbern
MATERIAL: Bone china
DATE: 2004
PHOTO: Dibbern

under the tutelage of ceramicist Richard Slee.

After graduation in 1997, Bodo exhibited as part of the New Designers exhibition in London where he was approached by the interior-design magazine *Wallpaper*. Hailed by the magazine as 'one of the designers to watch out for in the future', and also a year later having been awarded a Lord Sainsbury scholarship for free studio space at the OXO Tower, he began to gain support for his works and started up his design practice.

Now a trained ceramicist, Bodo was able to create pieces himself and commenced small-scale batch production in his kiln. The kiln is still in use today, though his works are now created by other means. However, without his initial hands-on skill for making work from scratch, his empathy for the material would not necessarily persist as it does in the work that is currently being produced under his name. Collections followed for Browns and Thomas Goode & Co. in London, as Bodo began to attract the more design-conscious audiences and retailers.

Inspiration stems from what he calls 'everyday life': a walk in the park, a walk to the studio — he sees and is inspired. Looking at his in-house collections (pieces designed, created and sold under the Bodo Sperlein name), it is obvious that inspiration stems from nature. Bodo likes to use his pieces to create environments and often works at creating families of products to tell a story.

One of his first clients, in 1999, was the German porcelain manufacturer Nymphenburg, and since his first commissioned collection Bodo has created work for a number of prestigious clients worldwide. He puts his success down to the ability to create bespoke collections which lean upon stories that are relevant to each client.

Today Bodo builds upon his design consultancy and draws on his designer-maker background to inspire his works and collaborations with other

clients. He has what he calls a 'happy marriage' between his working practice and his design consultancy, and works now as a multifaceted product designer. Now also designing for silver, wood and glass, he has clearly developed the ability to work with the limitations and possibilities of a range of materials in the creation of new works.

Bodo Sperlein's advice for the next generation of designers is as follows: 'For a designer to be successful depends on a variety of aspects. First and foremost to have a unique style and a good business head. You should know the marketplace on a global scale and think big from day one – don't limit your market just to your home country. The latter [the home market] is usually the easiest option, but it will not make you very interesting to global companies and brands, and indeed will make it harder for them to employ your services. Be multifunctional and try to create trends rather than to follow them.'

Above
TITLE: Niagara
Chandelier for Lladro.
MATERIAL: Porcelain
with fibre optics.
DATE: 2007
PHOTO: Lladro

The principles of KleinReid are the same as you would find in a studio pottery yet the differences are vast. The design world has entered the craft world through this hybrid studio.

KleinReid is a studio pottery based in New York comprising the talents of James Klein and David Reid. When you hear the words studio pottery, or if you ever do a Google search for studio pottery, the images and the stereotypes you will find could not be further from the truth of where this studio is positioned within the design world.

The principles are the same as you would find in a studio pottery yet the differences are vast. The design world has entered the craft world through this hybrid studio, which is making waves on both sides of the Atlantic. Contemporary attitudes are married with traditional aesthetics, hand-applied glazes and secret recipes intertwined with pure design and postmodern values. 'We both were drawn to the medium of ceramics in undergraduate school and ending up majoring in the subject. I

think for both of us it was a material attraction,' explains David.

The duo have been working together in the studio for over fifteen years, during which time their portfolio of ceramics and glassware has grown to become a sought-after commodity in the design world. Their works have attracted a following among museums, galleries and the celebrity world, all wanting to collect KleinReid's signature style of what they describe as 'refined forms, intricate details and sumptuous glaze'.

Creating glazes and surface applications is a key part of what makes KleinReid more individual than other ceramic companies. They have an ability to use batch production while retaining their studio pottery attitude. Having the knowledge of glaze and a hands-on understanding of their craft is clearly one of the attributes behind the success of this dynamic studio.

'We drew up business plans and developed our porcelain body and glazes while James was finishing grad school in 1993,' explains David. Their first studio was set up after graduation the same year and was based in Willamsburg, Brooklyn, New York.

Both potters draw inspiration from a myriad of sources, including the New York-based designer Eva Zeisel's 'playful search for beauty' (as they describe it). Zeisel became famous for her design philosophies and her hold on the ceramic world in the USA. Her work, which was synonymous with function and design, often abstracted forms from the natural

Left
TITLE: 'Applied' Collection
MATERIAL: Bisque porcelain with glazed interior
DATE: 2008
PHOTO: KleinReid

Opposite
TITLE: 'Eva' Line
MATERIAL: Matte glazed porcelain
DATE: 1999–2001
PHOTO: KleinReid

world. In the UK Eva became the Royal Designer for Industry, and her work is manufactured by Stoke-on-Trent manufacturers of cream ware, Royal Stafford. At the age of 101 her new collections for Royal Stafford saw her win the Classic Design Award in 2009.

It is no wonder that Eva is fuelling a new generation of designers' and in 1999 the duo approached her with a proposal to collaborate on a project with them. The result was a series of six curvaceous flower vases which were hand-produced by the studio. In 2002 the studio introduced tea and tableware collections which were then translated into blown crystal in 2004.

'All our "studio" porcelain is made in-house by us and our assistants. We also design for other companies, including Herman Miller, and create items for our line (prints and soft goods), which is something we don't produce ourselves. We've also just introduced a new series for our company, called Applied, which is our first venture into small-batch overseas production in China.'

Not being content with bridging craft and design, James and David have gone back to their roots with the series called StillLife, which brings sculpture and objets d'art into their cocktail of influences. This collection comprises an eclectic mix of vessels and other objects, some old and some new. It was designed to encompass two different approaches to manufacture: small-scale batch-produced ware and 'one of a kind' collections.

This studio pottery refuses to stand still and is evolving craft for a new audience of collector-buyers. Their collections continue to follow their own mantra: 'playful design, fine craftsmanship and lasting beauty'.

Their advice for the next generation of designers is, 'Follow your heart and create honestly – it's the only way you'll make anything unique, lasting and satisfying. If you are going to make it yourself, be sure you're paid well. Don't try and compete with other products on price. As long as your work is good and you support it well, it finds its own audience.'

Above

TITLE: Candlestick and Happy Prince Candelabra from StillLife collection
MATERIAL: Bisque porcelain
DATE: 2006
PHOTO: KleinReid

Nicola Malkin creates a marriage between objets d'art and studio pottery whilst fashioning work that could belong in Alice's Wonderland.

Her collections include giant-sized jewellery, pearl-beaded necklaces the size of a sofa and bracelets where the charms are the size of vases.

It is only when seeing her objects in the flesh, or against an object which reveals the scale of the piece, that you realise Nicola is not only challenging perspective but also ceramic batch production on a sculptural level. She explains: 'I love the possibilities that working with clay brings. Endless handbuilt and industrial techniques that require skill and commitment to master. A challenging, yet strangely satisfying material to explore.'

Nicola's collections are full of drama and theatre in both scale and subject matter. Each item is hand-produced, glazed, decorated and fired using slipcasting techniques to make one-off, limited-edition and large-scale ceramics for collectors and interior designers.

Given the nature of her work, it is no surprise to discover that her route into ceramics was a little unconventional. 'I wanted to work in theatre creating stage props and scenery but then on my foundation course was introduced to ceramics. I was attracted to the workshop. It seemed full of interesting bits and pieces. The tools, glaze tests and general mess appealed to me, as did the fact that no one else wanted to do it. I was one of two ceramics students that year.'

Through immortalising everyday objects, Nicola brings the observer closer to items which would normally be deemed ordinary. Her collections are as functional as an item of jewellery, the only difference being that hers is a jewellery for interiors. Indeed, how jewellery personalises the wearer is an important factor that Nicola embeds within her work. The client can select from a wide range including giant pineapples, gold locks and floral bombs, each making ironic use of familiar symbols.

'Although my work can be one-off pieces,' she says, 'my Giant Charm Bracelets have limited-edition charms sometimes made in batches. I am inspired by re-creating stories, both my own and other people's. I am also always intrigued by other people's jewellery – it usually has its own story to tell.'

Selected for the Crafts Council scheme Next Move, Nicola was able to develop her work and exhibit in galleries and exhibitions. In 2005 she was awarded the Crafts Council Development Grant, which enabled her to properly establish her practice and studio in Surrey, England.

In describing her work process, she explains: 'I work in small batches. There will only ever be ten of one kind of charm

Below

TITLE: Detail of American Lady's Charm Bracelet
MATERIAL: Earthenware and porcelain charms, brass chain
DATE: 2008
PHOTO: Stephen Laverty

made from a mould if it's slipcast or hand-built. There will always be something subtly different about each one, whether it's the colour, glaze or print, or because of how it was produced. With the giant necklaces, I'll produce many, many beads out of the same moulds (of different scales) but then once again put them together in such a way that each necklace is unique.'

Nicola's advice for aspiring designers is various. On the one hand, 'Photograph your work beautifully and professionally. This is vital for demanding press opportunities.' But equally, she advises, 'Don't be overly concerned with what is in design magazines – it can be distracting for your own work. Just make what comes naturally. I pay very little attention to other ceramics when looking for inspiration.' Also, 'Consider collaborations carefully, and keep your website and blog updated (I'm terrible for this). And finally, take every opportunity you can.'

Left
TITLE: Pregnant Virgin
Mary Charm
MATERIAL: Earthenware
with brass halo
DATE: 2008
PHOTO: Stephen Laverty

Right
TITLE: Giant Charm
Bracelet
MATERIAL: Earthenware
and porcelain charms,
brass chain
DATE: 2006
PHOTO: Nicola Malkin

NICOLA MALKIN

Anja Lubach's work combines sculpture and function in a way that makes the viewer want to question the manufacturing processes used to create her pieces.

Most of Anja Lubach's work is produced in porcelain, a clay that she describes as a blank canvas. Its smooth qualities and unique translucency allow the maker to replicate through the use of small sprigs and moulds the very fine detail of all kinds of objects and surfaces.

Anja was born in Germany and is a graduate of the Royal College of Art in London. After her course she worked at Rosenthal Ceramics in Germany on an industrial placement in which she was given access to the model-making departments as well as the factory floor to freely experiment and further develop her ideas. This experience energised her work and gave her an understanding of both production techniques and the limitations of working in porcelain.

Anja set up her designer-maker practice in 2001. Five years later she moved her studio to the Cockpit Arts Studios in London, which pride themselves on being 'the UK's only creative business incubator for designer-makers'.

Drama is important to her, and the interactions of her pieces with the spaces they inhabit are key. There are vessels in Anja's collection which contain row upon row of faces gazing at each other like an audience in the round, and made with reflective high-gloss glazed surfaces. Light and shadow falling on the collections causes the individual pieces to appear to move and interact with one another, whilst the translucency of the body of clay adds depth and detail to the forms.

'Material experimentation plays a key role in my work' explains Lubach.

'I might spend weeks just literally manipulating clay to see what kind of result I might get and then I develop ways of how I can integrate these details into 3D forms.'

Anja has begun to develop ceramics which use a process she calls 'printing in relief'. The process is similar to the traditional craft of 'sprigging' a term used for the application of press-moulded shapes onto ceramics made popular by the Jasperware of Wedgwood.

Anja strips bare this perfectionism and adds a raw edge of attitude by producing vessels with decorative details that appear to have moulded forms pushing through the body of the clay.

'I love decadent ceramics and try to produce contemporary takes on these objects. Working with porcelain requires a lot of problem solving, as it is a very restrictive material to work with and I enjoy pushing the material's limitations'.

Anja believes there is a maker in all of us, and how you tap into that creative energy is what

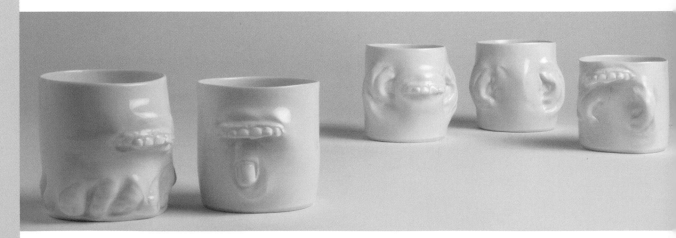

determines how it manifests. 'It became apparent to me as a young person that I would have to be in some way involved in the production and creation of objects of a kind. At first I nearly became a jeweller, but my hands and patience did not lend themselves to such small-scale work. When I had the chance to do some pottery, I fell in love with the process straightaway.'

Studio pottery that might be regarded as unconventional and in some cases frighteningly shocking plays a loose role in Anja's work. There is a definite sense of love it or hate it about her pieces. She uses the potter's wheel to create the basic vessel forms, which are then distorted and manipulated whilst still wet. She likes to set the uniformity of the thrown functional object against the irregularity of the vessel's altered surface. As she describes her own pieces, 'I see them as decorative objects to be viewed, discussed and cherished. They are containers of space, which might trigger memory and imagination.'

Her aim is quite simply 'to produce work which has a spontaneity and a seemingly effortless beauty', and this is evident within the fragile finished pieces, whose craftsmanship evokes simultaneously both purity and decadence. 'As I usually use porcelain and no added colour these visual opposites work in perfect harmony. I have recently developed a range in black sculptor's stoneware clay, which might be described as the perfect contrast to porcelain. There is no translu-

cency but a sense of creation and again metamorphosis in the details of faces squeezing through the craggy rough black vessel walls, their lack of functionality disabling the owner from using the forms in any way other than to display them, hence adding a further sculptural element.'

Anja's work is available from a number of galleries, and she exhibits at fairs such as Origin in the UK.

Her advice for new makers is, 'Be brave, be bold and be daring. It is a hard business to be in, and self-confidence is 50% of the success.'

Original ideas are supported by original forms which reflect Kathleen's passion for rituals, cultures and the passing down of traditions through the generations.

Kathleen Hills is a ceramics designer and maker. She celebrates modern and vintage design through her collections of tableware, lighting and kitchenware. She established her own studio in 2002 after first graduating from Central St Martins and then studying for an MA in ceramics and glass at the Royal College of Art.

Kathleen's work celebrates both the old and the new in design. Contemporary, organic and clinical forms are contrasted with traditional prints that have been fired onto the forms in a modernistic manner. She describes her work thus: 'I have a passion for conceptual thinking and narrative. I'm interested in how relationships are formed with objects within our domestic space.' Moreover, she says, 'My work often explores emotional attachments that exist with certain products or materials, products that explore inherited family tradition and culture or domestic ritual. I strive to combine the functionality of good design with the qualities of craft, technique and process.'

Kathleen's first exhibition was at 100% Design in 2003, at which she exhibited the work she continues to produce today. In 2004 she was selected to exhibit at Ambiente in Frankfurt, which helped her secure retail outlets, galleries and design boutiques through which her work could be sold to the general public.

Kathleen works mainly in slipcast bone china for its translucent qualities and thin casting properties. The use of this material, which was first developed in Britain, lends her pieces an air of preciousness while at the same time implicitly celebrating a significant aspect of British manufacturing history. 'I grew up in a manufacturing family, where instead of having prints hanging above the fireplace we had interesting wooden patterns and moulds for sand-casting metals. This gave me a real interest in British manufacturing and a genuine appreciation

of its importance. I believe manufacturing is an integral part of the design process. It is also a part I thoroughly enjoy.'

In 2005 Kathleen designed the Made in England rolling pin, a functional kitchenware product with a twist. The rolling pin has raised lettering on the surface of the bone china cylinder. When pastry is rolled using the pin, an imprint of the words 'made in england' is left behind in the dough. 'The inspiration for the Made in England rolling pin came to me whilst I was cooking with my son and niece. The design of this product attempts to celebrate inherited traditions and our nostalgia for them through the use of positive associations with contemporary products, materials and form.'

Her domestic lighting and tableware collections are predominantly manufactured in Stoke-on-Trent in England, still the hub of the ceramics industry in the UK.

One of her first pieces to go into production was the Milkii jug, closely followed by the Egg Cube and the Sugar Lump. These respectively are a double-necked milk bottle, an egg holder with integrated spoon rest and a platform partitioned to hold individual sugar cubes.

'I am interested in how relationships are formed with objects within our domestic spaces. My work often explores emotional attachments that exist with certain products or materials, products that explore

inherited family tradition and culture or domestic ritual. I find myself driven by achieving the functionality of good design with the qualities of craft, technique and process,' explains Hills.

Kathleen is a magpie for ingredients and combines second-hand objects within her work. In 2007 she designed the collection Vintage Tea Light which uses collected second-hand glass shades that are supported on a cylindrical bone china base. The result is a timeless yet whimsical collection which is reminiscent of 70s interiors yet brought into modern times and contemporary interiors.

'Supporting British manufacturing and using design in order to find sustainable means of development has always been very important to me. For this reason, I chose to manufacture my products in traditional, family-run companies in the UK. I think it's really important to meet the people you will be working with, so whatever manufacturing I need I visit and chat with them face to face. My manufacturers have always supported me and made sure the work was ready when I needed it, and also ironed out production problems.'

Kathleen's work is mainly produced using slip-cast bone china, although she also designs in materials such as earthenware, glass and Perspex among other media. She uses the manufactured forms as a base for applying hand-finishing techniques such as cut ceramic decals and paper cut-outs, bringing together manufacturing and craft in the process.

Her work can be found in design shops in Britain and in other countries, and she also sells through her own online retail boutique.

Kathleen's advice for the next generation of designers is, 'Start establishing press contacts while you are still studying. Go for sponsorships and competitions. Talk to various manufacturers, and work with the one you get on with best. Approach good stores and persuade them to use your products in their window displays. Finally, invest in some good photography or learn to take a good image yourself!'

Inspiration for designers is often retrieved from childhood. How you grow up and where you grow up are fundamental ingredients for the designer and the maker.

This statement could not be more true than in the case of this Czech Republic designer.

Maxim uses ceramics as his principal medium, and introduces glass, wax and found objects into the narratives of his facetious designs. He is the master of knowing how far boundaries can be pushed. His ideas are epigrammatic and his innovative designs, with their references to junk culture, suggest the pace of a life that could be lived in any modern metropolis. His experimentation is raw, his execution is fresh, and his ability to combine traditional values with modern design has inspired younger designers to try to follow suit. However, his take on modern culture comes from a perspective that only someone from the former Soviet Bloc could properly appreciate.

'I am a member of the last generation on this Continent that lived through Communism and its downfall and the transition to a democratic system that formerly was sometimes referred to by some people as capitalism. We were the last witnesses of the socialist system full of its communist ideals, which, however, after 40 years of this experiment were never fulfilled. During that time the adolescent generation (just like the others before them) longed for "something like" some form of freedom, but unlike our parents' generation, who longed for freedom of speech or the chance to travel freely, we wanted to drink cans of Coca-Cola and eat hamburgers at McDonald's.'

The Qubus Studio was set by Jakub Berdych in Prague in 2002, 13 years after the fall of Communism. Today, Maxim and Jakub are the designers behind the studio, which was set up to experiment and play with traditional manufacturing processes and the principal industries the Czech Republic was famous for, namely, ceramics and glass.

Maxim, as part of the new wave of designer-makers that emerged around that time, was drawn to the process of slipcast ceramics.

'Although I studied ceramics for eleven years from secondary school onwards, it was not until I was at the Academy of Arts in Prague that I made a porcelain pot. I found this process very special and very mysterious. Something that is liquid in the beginning turns into stone in the end.

'You have to respect so many limits, as porcelain is fired to nearly 1400°C (2550°F) and things just work the opposite way sometimes. For instance, to achieve a flat surface on the product you have to make it round on the model!

'I wanted to push this traditional material into new contexts, comment on our time, mass-produce our thoughts and distribute them onto home shelves around the world.'

In 2001, Maxim created a series of vessels called Cola Cup. Taking a cast from an existing cola bottle, he transformed the disposable plastic bottle into a ceramic cup, inspired by the throwaway culture of capitalism yet, through design, freezing in time an ironic memento to its ephemeral nature.

'Inspired by fast-food culture, the changing lifestyle on the path from Communism to capitalism, I began to cast sundry recyclable shapes. Amazed by their minimalism and fragile aesthetic, so close to porcelain, I began to create a collec-

tion for fast people who kept their services locked up in cupboards at home and spent their days in offices, consuming food from instant, single-use design. I was fascinated by the fact that, by a mere change of material, one could draw attention to a shape that people discarded every day. Inspired by a natural passion for DIY – the cut-off bottoms of PET (polyethylene terephthalate) bottles are a handy universal substitute for any kind of vessel – I cast a series of recyclable designs and suspended them in time, like fossils, in the noblest material of all – porcelain.'

This experimentation with materials, their transformation from the original source into ceramics, allowed Maxim to push his concept further. His drive to change cheap, everyday icons into objects of desire, beauty and prolonged life led to a series of iconic works which marked him out as a future star.

His first exhibition was in the year 2000, on a group stand at the Milan Furniture Fair. 'I immediately got offers, and someone from Habitat (for me then an unknown company) asked me if I produced my pieces industrially. I told them I didn't and they never got back to me. Anyway, when I came back to Prague I got another three offers and sold my idea! And that was probably the moment when I realised that ideas have to be exhibited so people can react!

Disposable food trays, containers and plastic cups have all been cleansed of their ordinary associations through being redesigned and reproduced by Maxim. In his series called Digi Clock the classical Czech carriage clock is immortalised through his

contemporary revision, in which the delicate hands of the clock are replaced with a crude digital timer which, as he describes, 'implants a futuristic display in the old-fashioned body. The display counts down the time and resembles an explosive, an aesthetic bomb that might damage your taste'.

The journey of Maxim, Jakub and Qubus Studio has led to changes and new opinions in design. Evolving the lifespan of objects and making them into something new is a continual process for the design duo, but most important is their hunger to see how far they can push us in accepting disposable objects, potential refuse, as objects of desire.

The work of Maxim and Jakub can be found in retail outlets, galleries and design boutiques worldwide, including The Design Museum in London, and they are represented and distributed in the UK by Thorsten van Elten (see Behind the Scenes, p.136).

Maxim's advice for the next generation of designers is this: 'When you make something, you need to know why you are making it and who the product is for. The viewer needs to be given answers through the design itself. Many people are unaware of the process and journey behind the product, but a good designer is able to encapsulate this within the piece.'

Above left
TITLE: Waterproof Vase
MATERIAL: Porcelain
DATE: 2002
PHOTO: Gabriel Urbanek

Above
TITLE: Little Joseph
MATERIAL: Porcelain
DATE: 2006
PHOTO: Gabriel Urbanek

Far left
TITLE: Cola Cup
MATERIAL: Porcelain
DATE: 2001
PHOTO: Gabriel Urbanek

Husband and wife duo Dominic and Frances Bromley are the designers behind Scabetti. Specialising in ceramic design, Scabetti's collections have received international critical acclaim.

The design studio of Scabetti was set up in 1999. Dominic and Frances were both educated in industrial design, which introduced them to product design with an orientation towards science and engineering. This background is evident in their approach towards product design and how they work with the characteristics of ceramics, making a feature of its translucency and the possibilities of cloning a form and reproducing it through the process of slipcasting.

After university, and with some years of design experience, Dominic began his own label Scabetti. Working from home, the creation of the pieces was not a problem, but the financial investment needed to promote and sell his work proved more difficult. In 1999, the Prince's Trust offered Dominic a small loan as well as a discount on stands at trade fairs such as Top Drawer in London. Scabetti has also been encouraged throughout its rise to prominence by UK Trade and Investment, the British European Design Group and the British Jewellery, Giftware and Finishing Federation.

Dominic grew up with ceramics, as his father John Bromley is a modeller and sculptor of fine bone-china figurines working for well-known companies such as Wedgwood and Royal Doulton. Dominic is keen to lean upon this family heritage in moving ceramics forward as a medium.

'When I set up Scabetti, the foremost aim was to produce sculptural objects. Initially I was thinking of working with a more modern material such as resin, but the feel just wasn't right. It was important to reproduce the designs in a material that had a more soulful quality to it,' explains Dominic. He soon realised that the slipcasting process commonly used to produce ceramic vessels offered an accessible method for small-scale batch production.

Scabetti's pieces stimulate the senses and are reminiscent in some contexts of a mid-20th century aesthetic. Early work such as the collection titled Amoeba lean upon sculpture from artists such as Barbara Hepworth, Henry Moore, Jean Arp and Alexander Calder.

Following a corporate career in design and design management, Frances is now a partner in Scabetti. The two like to retain an element of hands-on production whilst working in collaboration with the manufacturers, to ensure their creative minds are not compromised. Leaning upon their industrial design background, they are able to communicate their ideas to manufacturers from both a technological and craft-based platform.

Both Dominic and Frances find it difficult to categorise themselves under one job title. 'As a designer, the amount of time I actually spend designing is relatively small. We work predominantly with ceramics, but not exclusively, and although ceramics is my first love and the material I have most experience with, I don't have the knowledge that a studio potter would have, and so I don't regard myself as a ceramicist,' explains Dominic. 'What perhaps differentiates us from other ceramic makers is our approach. Not coming from a ceramics background means we tend to push the boundaries of what this material is capable of and how it's used.' They both constantly question as to why and how things are achieved and whether there is a 'different' way of producing them.

In 2003 Scabetti pursued the idea of suspending bone china on cables and created *Drawn to the Light*, followed later by *Shoal*, in which a dramatic cloud of fine bone-china fish circle a central light source.

Scabetti's advice is 'don't be too eager to set up in business by yourself. Both Fran and I worked in design-related industries before Scabetti, and the experience was and still is incredibly useful. Although it's wise to be aware of design trends, try to create work that you believe in – this doesn't necessarily mean always striving for originality, but a design that is the result of genuine passion tends to be stronger'.

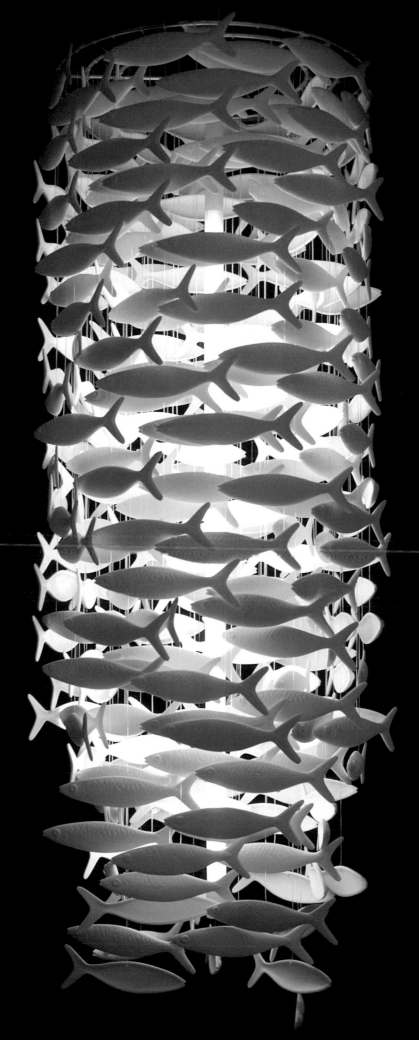

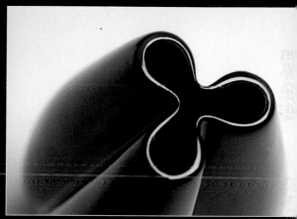

Top
TITLE: Cibola Pendant Light
MATERIAL: Bone china
DATE: 2006
PHOTO: Barrington Coombs
Above
TITLE: Tall Vase (detail)
MATERIAL: Earthenware
with black glaze
DATE: 2004
PHOTO: Courtesy of
Scabetti.
Left
TITLE: Shoal 284
MATERIAL: Bone china
DATE: 2007
PHOTO: Mark Wood

33

History is often revisited through trend, and one of the most significant foundations in the creation of trends is that of furniture. Through form and function these movable objects dictate our lifestyles, provide energy and relaxation and have historically created environments with a clear sense of purpose. Interior designers and architects once specified furniture that would be hard-wearing, basic and harsh to the eye, for use in doctors' waiting rooms and public spaces. Wipe-down, short-stay, uncomfortable and sterile furniture found its way into public spaces and it was only the home where comfort and design mattered. Even cafes provided furniture offering function over comfort, and metal became the choice of proprietors over traditional materials such as wood and textiles. We then saw the boom of the brown leather sofa, which cloned a certain idea of comfort in many homes and worked perfectly with beige walls. Perhaps we even owe gratitude to the US sitcom, Friends, which changed the coffee shop into an extension of the home as the sofa moved out of the lounge and into waiting rooms and cafes.

Today our response to design is changing, and materials are more exposed in the design of works which pay homage to childhood memories and nature rather than the need to accommodate bums on seats. Boutique hotels, restaurants, bars and coffee houses are turning to furniture to carve out their identities and become destinations in which to unwind and recharge.

Sustainability plays an important role in contemporary design, and this is most explored through furniture. Using products which leave a lasting footprint through design rather than manufacture is at the heart of many designs, whilst materials are used which have less impact on the environment.

The furniture designer is a materials empathiser and a constructionist playing with materials.

Opposite
TITLE: Anne Table and Chair
ARTIST: Gareth Neal
MATERIALS: American walnut
DATE: 2007 table/2009 chair
PHOTO: Damian Chapman and Ian Forsyth

Based in a small village in Leicestershire, furniture designer Eiry Rock's studio is very similar to her work: space-conscious, with each area having a purpose or function.

Eiry Rock sketches regularly to work out dimensions and detailed drawings on paper before transferring them onto CAD files.

Eiry calls herself a furniture designer-maker. Combining the sketchbook with the workshop is important to Eiry, as is her drive to carve a career as a furniture designer who tackles social interaction around the table. As she puts it, 'I hope to bring more awareness to the consumer demand for high-end design products, particularly for children, and meet that demand with suitable and affordable design solutions.'

After graduating Eiry gained hands-on knowledge of the way traditional furniture is made. She worked at a bespoke furniture maker in Leicester, which helped her gain a better understanding of the conventional manufacturing processes, thus supporting her strong belief that hands-on, traditional craft skills should have a place in the modern world. She applies these skills to pieces of furniture whose innovative elegance is also functionally astute. 'I have focused my attention on creating a visual balance within a usable end product which would not be visually or functionally complete without all components in place.'

Unusual juxtapositions of structural elements are a feature of Eiry's work. 'My work addresses the relationship objects share with each other and their dependency upon one another,' she says, 'whilst being an expression of form and simplicity.'

This is nowhere more apparent than in the furniture piece she calls Box Chair (see photo opposite), a child's chair and table in which for easy storage the different parts fit together like a puzzle. Indeed, this piece earned her the Hub Innovation Prize (Centre of Craft and Design, Lincolnshire) alongside Design Factory's Designer of the Year award in 2007.

Eiry describes all of her works and furniture pieces as functional, an element that is always of key importance to her when designing. But the sculptural elements within the furniture mean it would not look out of place in a gallery. In fact, this eye-catching quality is part of the point. 'Day-to-day objects are often taken for granted,' she says. 'I want to move away from this notion within my work and make people aware of what's in front of them.'

Eiry is an observer of people and social interaction. Her work is informed by the visual research she carries out, recording how people interact, talk and live with each other, and how furniture is used. The interaction between human being and object is obviously important. In recent projects she has been concentrating upon making furniture for children, and studying how child and parent interact with one another through the use of furniture. In these pieces, height and scale play an important role, as in the Pivoting Chair, as too does simplicity and function.

Box Chair Storage, (an adaptation of Box Chair/Child's Chair) represents a pure solution combining storage with a work surface. The inclusion of a child's chair within the piece offers the possibility of interaction between adult and child, while the notion of tidying up after play has been a source of inspiration for the overall design.

Left

TITLE: Pivoting Chair
MATERIALS: 50mm
(2in.) ash
DATE: 2007
PHOTO: Courtesy of
Loughborough
University

Eiry's works, such as the Pivoting Chair, Slot Seating and Utility Unit, are mainly produced in timber, though they also incorporate fibreboards, laminates and veneers. Moreover, the sourcing and use of materials is an important consideration when designing a piece. 'I source timber from well-managed forests and always ask about its origins when ordering. I also look out for the FSC symbol on all relevant materials. The sustainability of the manufacturing process is also something that is important to me. I veer away from designing polluting products, and I savour every piece of waste material for future projects or timber recycling.'

Eiry's advice for the next generation of designers is, 'Think carefully about your products and how they tie in with consumer demands. I would advise you to structure a business plan detailing your aims over a set period of time and to try to stick to that plan whilst being open-minded to unforeseen opportunities. Above all, have confidence and faith in your products, and promote them effectively.'

Left
TITLE: Box Chair/Child Chair
MATERIALS: 50mm (2in.) ash, 12mm (0.5in.) MDF, paint
DATE: 2007
PHOTO: Courtesy of Loughborough University

Above
TITLE: Flip Chairs
MATERIALS: 30mm (1.25in.) American black walnut, 15mm ($^5/_8$ in.) MDF, American walnut veneer
DATE: 2008
PHOTO CREDIT: Eiry Rock

Clinical and contemporary forms are balanced through Marina's ability to marry materials with function based upon the piece's interaction with the end user.

Marina Bautier is a furniture designer who works from her studio in Brussels on collaborations with manufacturers and interior projects for private clients, and also creates her own collections for spaces and places. Marina set up the studio in 2003, after her first exhibition at the Salone Satellite (a showground for young and emerging designers) in Milan in 2001.

Her work uses materials for their purity and their inherent characteristics. Clinical and contemporary forms are balanced through Marina's ability to marry materials with function based upon the piece's interaction with the end user. 'I am interested in the use of a product and the way furniture builds up space and behaviour, or brings a response in our behaviour.'

Marina makes her first pieces or prototypes herself before working with skilled craftspeople to produce the final collections. 'When making the prototypes, I get part of the pieces made here in Belgium by craftsmen or by industry. For the production I then work with several manufacturers, such as Ligne Roset in France, Idée in Japan, De La Espada in Portugal and Case in the UK.'

Case, established in 2006, is an award-winning furniture company set up by Sheridan Coakley (founder of SCP) and Paul Newman (founder of Aero and INK). Paul and Sheridan have both worked in the furniture industry for over 20 years and have actively encouraged some of the most prolific furniture names by representing and manufacturing their work.

Marina has worked with Case on her storage and shelving concept entitled Lap, a collection designed to offer low production costs, and to be space-efficient while interacting with the consumer by adapting to the particular needs of the user through the use of movable shelves, storage containers and platforms.

In 2009 Marina created a design for modular

seating. A solid oak frame is used to create the seats, which are redolent of a doctor's surgery waiting room, while a tall, elegant black steel floor lamp is fixed to one side. As day turns into dusk, the light from the lamp offers a halo of warmth that complements the oak and transforms the seating into a domestic item, a place for reading books and recovering from hectic lifestyles.

'I like to work hands-on,' she says, 'to be able to understand the materials I use and to test the function of a product I'm working on. I am inspired by daily life and the things we do each day around the house.'

Recovery and relationship are important to Marina. The work she produces seems to assist the end user in making life more simple, but her simplicity offers elegance and fuels conversation.

In 2008 she created the chair design entitled Fold (see opposite). There are influences here from the designer and architect Ludwig Mies van der Rohe, famous for the creation of the Barcelona Day Chair which cannot go unrecognised. Her passion for making life easier for us leads to this design being collapsible and foldable, much like a deckchair, but with Marina's signature for high design, craftsmanship and sophistication.

Marina's advice for future designers is, 'Be curious, and observe what surrounds you. It takes time for work to mature and to find the right people to collaborate with, so stay confident. Trust your own ideas, and work at your own rhythm. Enjoy your work!'

Above
TITLE: Frames
MATERIAL: Glass, oak and MDF
PHOTO: Courtesy of the artist

Below
TITLE: Armchair
MATERIAL: Solid oak, polyurethane foam, kvadrat polyester fabric, plywood and steel
PHOTO: Courtesy of the artist

Opposite page, left
TITLE: Chaise
MATERIAL: Solid oak
PHOTO: Courtesy of the artist

Opposite, right
TITLE: Fold
MATERIAL: Lacquered steel, polyurethane foam and wool
PHOTO: Courtesy of the artist

'We always aim to design functional designs with strong silhouettes which give an object a distinctive, simple and recognisable aesthetic.'

Natalie Cole graduated in 2001 and Wayne Pottinger in 2002, both with an MA in furniture design and technology. Pottinger and Cole explore the potential in combining handmade approaches with manufacturing techniques, whilst pushing the boundaries to create objects which are striking in design and challenging in their makeup. Nevertheless, their attitude towards design is both humorous and simple, and their objects can't fail to bring a dash of drama and wit to conventional interiors.

Their 'self-production' approach to design allows them to make work themselves at their own workshop whilst also forming links with manufacturing sources where necessary. The result of this mix of self-reliance and partnership creates a balance of production methods which clearly not only stimulates their own designs but adds an element of exploration to their design process through combining handmade with machine-made methods. 'We have been taking inspiration from manufacturing capabilities – not always necessarily hi-tech manufacturing processes – and working within the constraints of a simple production process.'

'We always aim to design functional designs with a strong silhouette', Wayne says. Indeed, the duo's interest in silhouettes and shadow was overtly explored in a series of powder-coated metalwork

Left
TITLE: Twiggi coat stand
MATERIAL: Mild Steel
DATE: 2006
PHOTO: Pottinger & Cole

Right
TITLE: Segment nest of tables
MATERIAL: MDF and plywood
DATE: 2006
PHOTO: Pottinger & Cole

accessories that includes Twiggi and Branch, a self-produced coat stand and coat hook respectively, which bring the outside inside through the use of silhouettes of trees and birds.

In 2007 they were shortlisted for the New Designers Award, and in 2008 were granted the Crafts Council Development Award to further their practice. Today Pottinger and Cole continue working with materials and manufacturing processes in what Wayne explains as exploring 'economic outcomes'. The result is a series of new collections which include lighting, accessories and furniture to be launched at 100% Design and unveiled as part of the 2010 London Design Festival. Their aim is to make products with an awareness of the environment whilst making the work affordable, enabling them to bring their craft, design and product to a wider audience.

Their advice for the next generation of designers is, 'Work hard. Make the most of opportunities. Have short-term and long-term goals to work towards. Know your market. Work hard (again).'

Below

TITLE: Invert coffee table
MATERIAL: Rolled mild steel with glass top
DATE: 2008
PHOTO: Pottinger & Cole

The main inspiration behind Gareth's work is material and process, a case of 'blurring boundaries and using historical narratives'.

Gareth Neal graduated in 1996 and like many of his peers his first exhibition was New Designers at the Business Design Centre in London. In 1997 he exhibited pieces as part of the Contemporary Decorative Arts Exhibition at Sotheby's in London. His business was launched with support from the UK government-funded Business Link, and he was also the beneficiary of a start-up loan from the Princes Youth Business Trust, now called The Prince's Trust.

What makes Gareth unique is his approach towards wood as a medium, which combines craft, design, art and function. It is clear that experimenting and playing with his material has been an important element in the development of his iconic furniture. 'I was first introduced to the material as a child while I was playing with offcuts as my dad did some DIY,' he explains. 'Wood as a material has always appealed, with its natural smells, colours and textures.'

Gareth set up his furniture design practice in 2003, and he mainly specialises in one-off pieces, with the clients ordering his designs both nationally and internationally.

The main inspiration behind Gareth's work is material and process, a case of 'blurring boundaries and using historical narratives', as he puts it. 'The work tries to engage with the viewer and create inter-sector debate amongst art, design and craft, between history and the contemporary, between the material and the immaterial.'

A good example of this debate is his console table entitled Anne. Solid blocks of wood used to make the basic shape of a Queen Anne-style console table are sliced into using hundreds of thin parallel saw cuts to varying depths, revealing the more ornate silhouette of an authentic Queen Anne-style table, complete with apparently turned cabriole legs. As this ghostly image appears through the wood, a dichotomy emerges between the contemporary outer shell, harsh-edged and

Above
TITLE: Anne Table
MATERIAL: American walnut
DATE: 2007
PHOTO: Damian Chapman and Ian Forsyth

Right
TITLE: Anne Chair
MATERIAL: American walnut
DATE: 2009
PHOTO: Ian Forsyth

Opposite, top
TITLE: Capillary Side Table
MATERIAL: Oak
DATE: 2008
PHOTO: Damian Chapman

minimal, and the classic piece that dwells within, a harmony with tradition and heritage which seems to grow from the core of the object.

The console table was preceded by a piece entitled George III, a chest of drawers that followed the same principles of design. Gareth used the same process of slicing away the timber with the blade of the saw to reveal the ornate and curvaceous form of a Georgian original.

The work is made through a mixture of mechanical and human intervention which Gareth balances perfectly. His unique combination of high-quality craftsmanship, 3D computer-drawing skills and computer-numerical-controlled (CNC) processes has pushed his work into distinctive new areas.

He designs and makes all the pieces himself, with only some aspects of the manufacturing process, such as the CNC routering, needing to be outsourced.

The relationship between an object and the maker behind the object is important to Gareth. In 2009 he held his solo show entitled 'Made to View' at the Contemporary Applied Arts Gallery in London. One of the highlights of this one-man show was Gareth himself, who transformed the gallery into a workshop whilst he recreated his designs as though it were a performance piece for visitors to the gallery – illustrating not only the making processes behind the furniture but exposing the maker behind the creations.

Gareth has exhibited his work at 100% Design in London, Origin, also in London, and at SOFA in Chicago (one of the venues for the international exhibition for Sculpture, Objects and Functional Arts, held in Chicago, New York and Santa Fe). He continues to produce work which is empathetic to the past whilst celebrating the present.

Gareth's advice for the next generation of designers is, 'Take it seriously. Be prepared for

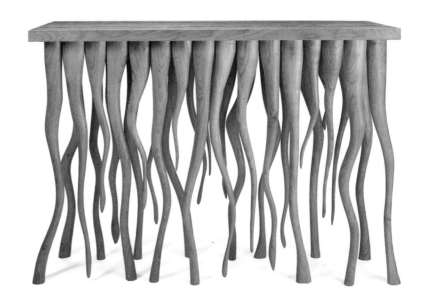

hard work. Make sure you get the costing correct. Be prepared to have to do other things to pay the bills, and finally remember that "the dog that stays on the porch finds no bones!"'

Below
TITLE: George
MATERIAL: Oak
DATE: 2008
PHOTO: James Champion

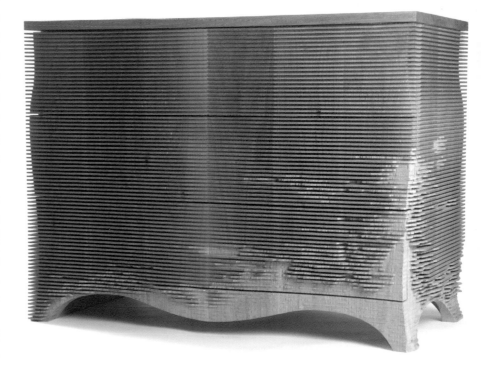

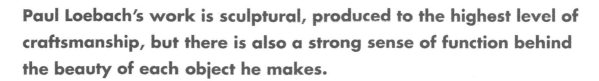

Paul Loebach's work is sculptural, produced to the highest level of craftsmanship, but there is also a strong sense of function behind the beauty of each object he makes.

Paul works with his strengths when producing a piece of work, but he also understands his limitations when more methods are needed. 'I make pieces myself using traditional woodworking when I can. I work with factories when the project calls for advanced machining.'

He classes himself as a designer-artist, a description which fits the work perfectly, as this is what he does: creates art with design. 'I'm inspired by traditional materials, new manufacturing technologies, innovative design processes, cultural history and decorative arts,' he explains, 'I also look at philosophy and post-structuralism, semiotics and the meaning of everyday objects.'

Paul shows an appreciation and a passion for both traditional craftsmanship and for state-of-the-art manufacturing process. He appears to want to underline that one way is no more influential than the other in determining design outcomes.

'I'm inspired by the history of manufacturing and the symbolic meaning of our material world,' he explains. 'I'm fascinated with crafts and decorative objects from all times and places. My greatest inspiration comes from the curious and humble objects that people collect for their special personal meanings. The form of my designs comes from my drive to push the limits of what a given material can do, and to challenge what we are conditioned to recognise as "normal" – I'm searching for the exact point at which something familiar becomes special.'

He describes his Wood Chair, which is made from solid maple, as 'lavish 18th-century-inspired turnings meet clean minimalism head-on'. The piece was made by a French chairmaker living in Brooklyn, Paul's home borough in New York City.

Another piece that shows this passion for crossing distinctions between design, craft and fine art is the collection entitled Vase Space (see opposite). According to Paul, the inspiration for this work, in which a side table gives the illusion of having three vases growing from its tabletop, comes from 'American federal furniture and the obsessive nature of neo-classicism'.

In fact, although the whole ensemble seems to have been turned as one extraordinary piece, the vases are all removable.

His advice for new designers and furniture

makers is, 'Work hard and be true to your vision. Ignore what everyone says and stay focused. Finally, of course, be prolific!'

Far left
TITLE: Step Stools
MATERIAL: Hard maple, birch plywood
DATE: 2008
PHOTO: Jeremy Frechette

Below
TITLE: Vase Space
MATERIAL: Hard maple
DATE: 2008
PHOTO: Jeremy Frechette

This image
TITLE: Half Mirror
MATERIAL: Basswood, low-iron glass
DATE: 2008
PHOTO CREDIT: Jeremy Frechette

Left
TITLE: Wood vases
MATERIAL: Machined maple
DATE: 2009
PHOTO: Jeremy Frechette

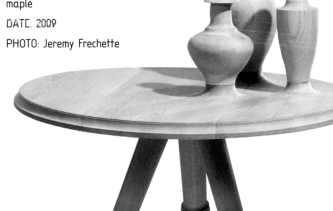

'I spend so much of my time experimenting and trying new things out. I love doing this and it often results in the creation of a new product.'

Tom Raffield's approach to design seems simple: using traditional processes with a twist of the imagination whilst pushing processes and the manipulation of materials to extremes. The results are pieces of furniture which will inevitably take their place alongside those of history's most recognised designers and become part of our own design heritage.

Tom graduated from Falmouth College of Arts in 2005, where he studied 3D design for sustainability. It was in the second year of his course that Tom experimented with different ways of manipulating and forming wood. He was introduced to the process called 'steam-bending' and, as he explains, 'was amazed by its potential'.

It was in 1859 that the designer Michael Thonet mastered the use of steam-bent wood to create masterpieces of furniture including the iconic Thonet bentwood chair. In later years the architect Le Corbusier hailed the chair as a landmark in engineering, and remarked, 'Never has anything been created more elegant and better in its conception, more precise in its execution, and more excellently functional.'

Whilst it would probably be unjustified to make a similar claim for Raffield's work, especially at this early stage in his career, nevertheless there is a classic air about his pieces that stems from the same purity of conception found in the Thonet chair.

'Thonet has been a huge inspiration to me and how my work has developed, especially in the earlier years,' Tom explains. 'It almost felt as though steam-bending was a lost art, used in its most basic form with no one pushing the process forward or doing anything new with it.'

Tom is using the same techniques that were used by his predecessors, such as Thonet, to create furniture, lighting and installations that, although paying homage to the past, are also strikingly contemporary.

In January 2006, immediately after graduating, Tom launched a design practice called Sixixis with two other college friends, and it wasn't long before the company had won a number of awards, including the Laurent Perrier Design Talent Award 2006. These led to exhibitions such as 100% East in London and to showcasing new works at Origin, the annual international craft fair run by the Crafts Council, also held in London.

In 2008 Tom moved away from the security and shared umbrella of a joint design venture to continue his career and create new collections under his own name and company Tom Raffield Design. Now a sole designer, he retains his passion for creating new works which require him to be both the designer and the manufacturer.

He has been busy working on new collections designed exclusively for Cornish furniture and lifestyle brand MARK (a design manufacturer championing the skills of craftsmen working in Cornwall in England). He has created a design called the Ribbon Light for them, which uses his trademark bentwood processes in the form of a pendant light. This was shortlisted for the Homes and Gardens lighting award in 2009. Tom is aware of what his potential clientele is looking for when purchasing his designs. Each chair he makes is numbered, dated and signed by him to underline that what the client is buying is something far removed from the kind of furniture that can be bought on the high street, with the designer being also intimately involved in the manufacturing process. 'I love the making side, and seeing a product through from beginning to end,' he says, 'so I make sure all the products made are mainly made by myself or at least under my supervision.'

When asked about the main inspiration behind his works, Tom explains, 'It is a bit of a cliché, but where I live and the natural environment has a big impact on my work. I spend so much of my time experimenting and trying new things out. I love doing this and it often results in the creation of a new product.'

Although Tom is a relatively new designer, his work is so strong that his career will surely go from strength to strength. His advice for new designers is clear: 'Be prepared. Write a good business plan to really understand how your business is going to work. Get as much relevant work experience as possible before starting. Share a space with other

Above
TITLE: Ash Pendant No. 1
MATERIAL: FSC–certified ash
DATE: 2008
PHOTO: Mark Wallwork

like-minded people to cut costs. Share equipment and bounce ideas off one another. Talk to people in the industry so you can understand as much as possible, so you know what you are letting yourself in for. And finally, surround yourself with people who can help you: a business mentor, an accountant, a buyer for a retail outlet – whoever can give you free advice and help.'

Far left
TITLE: Chaise Longue no. 4
MATERIAL: English oak
DATE: 2007
PHOTO: Mark Wallwork

Right
TITLE: Rocking Chair
MATERIAL: English ash with leather upholstered seat
DATE: 2007
PHOTO: Mark Wallwork

TOM RAFFIELD

47

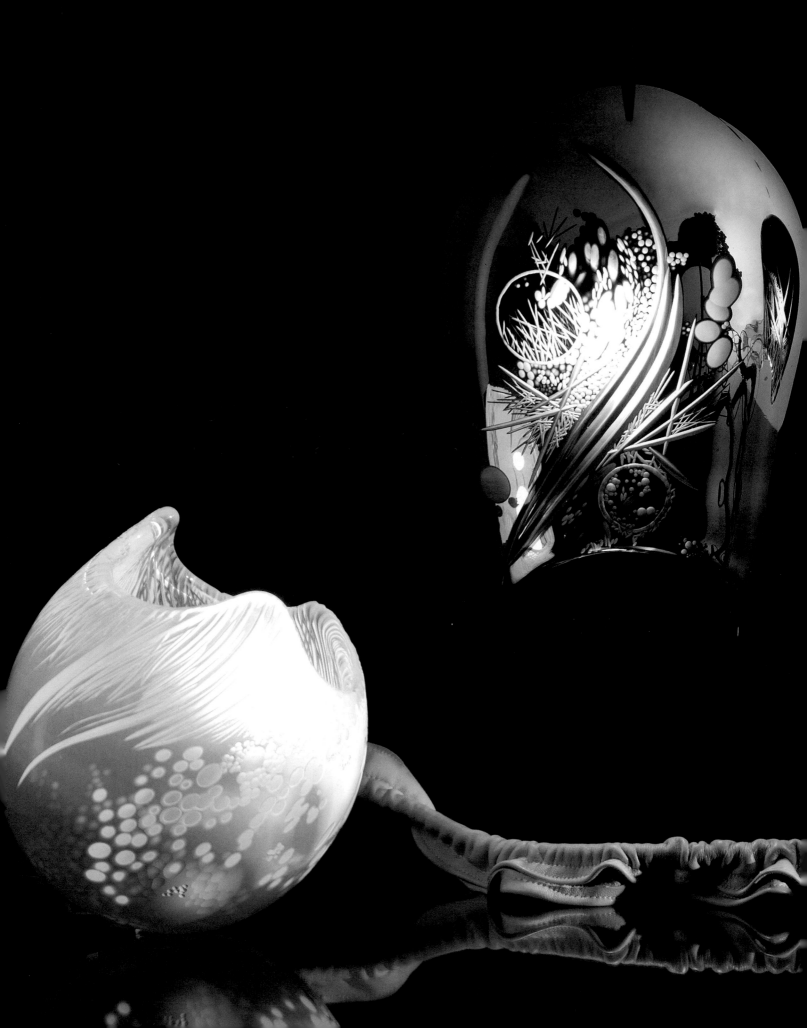

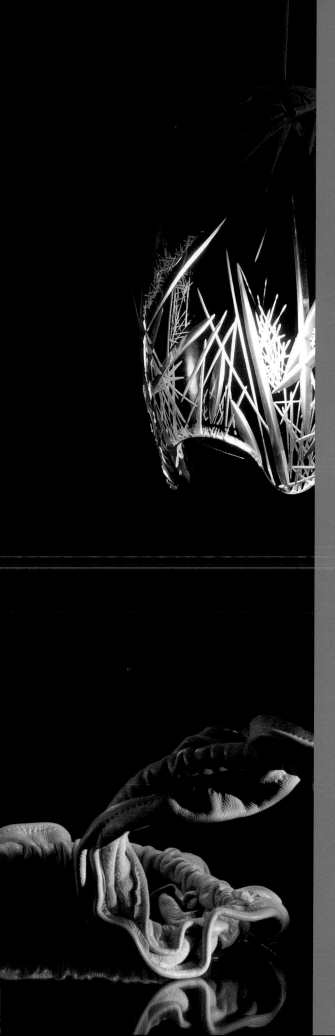

Glass

The design and production of glass demands a great deal of crafsmanship and skill to take on the material's limitations and methods of manufacture. A blown piece of glass is as much about the creator as it is about the object. As with most craft forms, this skill is often passed from generation to generation through the processes of slumping, fusing, blowing and kiln forming now taught through university courses and studio workshops. It is these skilled craftsmen and women who are passing on the baton of knowledge containing ourindustrial heritage, whilst creating a breeding ground for new audiences. It is this synergy of heritage and design which today's craftspeople are fusing together in the creation of conversation pieces for homes and interiors.

The glassmaker has at their disposal the ability to create using free-form and mould-formed processes of production. Add to this the application of surface design through sand-blasting, diamond cutting and engraving, and it is not difficult to see why glass and glassware passing through the hands of the contemporary craft maker are reacting with the consumer like never before.

Lighting is being challenged through read-dressing the chandelier, and the artisan is fusing with the designer in creating centrepieces that encapsulate every move, mark and breath of the maker in the final object and design.

Glass offers a time capsule in which the designer can capture inspiration from fashion, design and craft. Designers are creating fossils depicting our current habitats, lifestyles and environments. Nature plays an important role for many designers, but today's glass contemporaries are looking further afield and trapping our emotions, human chaos, as well as our design past and present, in each and every piece.

Opposite

TITLE: Break the Pattern lighting

ARTIST: Heather Gillespie

DATE: 2008

PHOTO: Tas Kprianou

Anu Penttinen works as a freelance designer within the Finnish glass industry and also as a maker under her own business name, Nounou Design.

Her work fuses together bold colours, lines and patterns with organic free-flowing forms that stand out in any setting. Blacks, reds and whites nestle themselves in patterns on architectural vessels, whilst lime-greens, lemons, oranges and reds make for mouth-watering opposites in candy-inspired objects. Indeed, opposites tend to attract in her portfolio of vessels, bowls, paperweights, wall art, lighting and sculptures. 'I am intrigued by the relationship between order and disorder,' she says, 'and how these can be translated, through personal journeys, into the glass material.'

In 2003 she set up a studio and workshop in Finland, where she is based today. Anu now has her studio in the Nuutàjarvi glass village. The Nounou dsign studio and shop are located today in this Finnish glass centre where glass first started in 1793. 'I started my business due to practical reasons,' explains Anu. 'I had never thought of having my own business during my studies. There wasn't very much information out there about being an entrepreneur, and I have learned everything the hard way. Making glass was my initial goal, and starting the business just made certain things easier for me and my clients. It took me one year to start the business after graduation, and I also worked as a full-time glass lecturer to finance my business.'

Anu's first show was at Beaver Galleries in Canberra, Australia, which introduced her to the idea of selling work in gallerys. The show was a success and she decided that 'I could make a living in art glass'.

As a freelance designer Anu has worked with Sarner Crystal in Switzerland and the famous design house Iittala, where in 2008 she was asked to create a new collection of Professor Oiva Toikka's 'birds' which are a treasured part of Finnish life and glass-making heritage. The birds are a symbol of not only traditional values but of traditional craft, something which Anu perfectly illustrates within her own work.

Anu works with glass-blowing, kiln-forming and cold-working techniques to create pieces for homes, interiors and public/architectural spaces. Collections are small-scale and batch-produced, and are designed in families or 'project groups' under a single title in order to create a wide selection of glass objects with shared characteristics. This offers collectors the chance to buy one-off statement pieces as well as offering more commercially viable work to wider audiences at lower price points.

Opposite page
TITLE: Urban Box Nos 1–4
MATERIAL: Base –
handblown and wheel–cut
glass; Top – fused and
wheel–cut glass
DATE: 2008
PHOTO: Courtesy of the artist

Anu produces everything marketed under the Nounou Design name herself, and sells her work across the globe to galleries, retailers and collectors. She is creating collectables for a modern generation, drawing inspiration from the typical hectic modern lifestyle, which she describes as 'both urban and sub-urban – with its signs, traffic, lights, noise and maps'.

Her advice for the next generation of glass designers is, 'Create your own distinctive and recognisable style/technique/concept. Follow your own chosen path with confidence – it will be noticed. Say yes to any possible chance to be noticed, marketed, collaborated with – even the smallest exhibition, event or fair stand can bring along something new. Invest in promoting oneself and making yourself visible to different audiences. Work as hard as it takes to create first-class quality, and don't settle for anything less.'

Below
TITLE: Detour No. 5
MATERIAL: Handblown,
wheel–cut and engraved
glass
DATE: 2009
PHOTO: Courtesy of the artist

Below
TITLE: Maze No. 13
MATERIAL: Fused and kiln-formed glass
DATE: 2009
PHOTO: Courtesy of the artist

Kathryn says her inspiration stems from textiles and fashion in the world around her, 'resulting in an explosion of colour, pattern, texture, image and text'.

Kathryn is a relatively young glass artist and maker, yet the period of time she has spent in education has contributed to both her development as an artist and the level of research she puts into materials. After graduating in glass and ceramics from the University of Sunderland in 2004, she continued her studies by taking an MA in Glass, and in 2010 is due to complete her Ph.D., which explores the development of hot glass and print.

Her work tells stories and incorporates hidden messages which contribute to the fine-art aesthetic of her vessels, bowls and other structures. There is also an element of humour in these playful pieces, and an uncompromising ability to contrast colour with texture. 'The introduction of print into my work has given me the opportunity to communicate with my audience using my own narrative. For example, the series of work I produced for my MA was entitled 'forgive me father for I have sinned'. This series was a modern-day twist on an ancient concept – the seven deadly sins – with comic-strip-style imagery trapped in layers of glass. Each glass vessel detailed one of the sins.'

In November 2005, Kathryn was selected for the Next Move Placement, which is hosted by the Crafts Council. 'This was a joint undertaking between the University of Sunderland and the Crafts Council. The aim of the placement was to establish my own practice. It offered both support and financial help. In 2006 I received a grant from the Arts Council to establish my business.'

In 2008, Kathryn produced a black and white collection entitled 'opposites attract', comprising oval forms with contrasting interiors and exteriors. Their screenprinted surfaces are set against cut and polished edges and other, plain surfaces, offering a contrast between purity and decoration. 'Seeing is believing...', on the other hand, is the title of a series of brightly coloured capsules comprising sleek black exteriors which have been hand-blown with subtle hues of orange, purple, blue, yellow, olive-green and pink.

Kathryn explains, 'I have developed an innovative technique based on layering screenprinted transfers and sandblasted patterns, and more recently flocked detailing, to create a range of beautifully simple yet challengingly complex forms'.

Kathryn is creating a seductive portfolio of glass that draws inspiration from modern times. Her collections reflect today rather than the past, and encapsulate fresh artistic approaches whilst reflecting modern times. She is clearly an artisan who is simultaneously bridging craft, fashion and design, and in doing so is playing a leading role for the next generation of glassmakers.

Above
TITLE: Flocking Hell!
MATERIAL: Blown glass forms and polished rims with white and yellow flocked palm tree
DATE: 2007
PHOTO: Tas Kyprianou

The advice she offers to the next generation of designer-makers is to 'Get out there and get your name known. You should have long-term goals — deciding what you want to achieve and when you want to achieve it by — and constantly review your progress and your goals.

'Good planning and time management are essential — not just looking at what is happening next week but also looking at what is happening next month and even next year. You need to plan ahead.

'Make the most of every opportunity that comes along, however big or small. The more you get your name out there, the more people will remember you. Make sure that all images of your work are produced by a professional photographer. It is the good images that are chosen for publicity in books and magazines — if your images look great you will benefit from free publicity.

'Finally, trust your instincts and never give up: however bad it may seem there is always something else around the corner. If you are confident you will succeed.'

Stuart Akroyd is a glassmaker who takes his inspiration from nature, creating the sensation of movement and fluidity in a solid form.

Stuart's signature style is a blend of asymmetry and vibrant colours, striking patterns and shapes, much of which is inspired by the waters of the Caribbean. At the beginning of Stuart's career it was with help from the Enterprise Allowance Scheme (a government initiative of the1990s) that Stuart was able to set up his own cold-working studio, whilst hiring facilities for his hot-shop work. Since 2000, Stuart has been able to expand his business and now works from his workshop in Nottinghamshire which houses his furnace and three glass kilns.

Through trade exhibitions and fairs Stuart has built up a customer base to whom he sells through prestigious retail outlets and galleries. He also sells direct to the public through high-quality events such as Origin: the London Craft Fair.

His work is tactile and timeless, and showcases his experience and skill for creating craft with lasting appeal. The intention is simple: to offer pieces for all who appreciate craft skills and objects of beauty and the skills needed to make them. Through his production pieces he is able to ensure that work is accessible to different audiences whilst his limited editions offer the collector exclusivity and unique approaches to finishing and polishing as well as the assurance provided by a certificate of authenticity.

Stuart is creating collectables which may well become the heirlooms of tomorrow, channelling skill and craftsmanship into the making of an object for a new generation. His one-off pieces are made using the *encalmo* technique where the glass is twice-blown; cups are made, cooled and then decorated and multiples of these cups are then reheated and joined together to create the final form. This is his adaptation of a traditional Venetian technique, which illustrates his technical abilities and contribution to the world of glassmaking.

Stuart is proud of the fact that he has always designed and blown his own work. The very nature of hot glassmaking requires an assistant, but with increased demand for his work he has also employed assistants for cold-finishing and preparing the glass for delivery. 'It is integral to my work that I have a hands-on approach, as the design process only begins on paper and continues through making.'

Stuart's advice for the next generation of designers is, 'Don't design yourself out of any profit — remember that this is a business.

Left

TITLE: Joom Vase Closed

MATERIAL: Seven piece encalmo–blown vase

DATE: 2007

PHOTO: Tim Spriddell

Right

TITLE: Sirl Decanter

MATERIAL: Encalmo glass decanter

DATE: 2008

PHOTO: Tim Spriddell

Below

TITLE: Cirfunkerance Bowl

MATERIAL: Twice–blown bowl with hot
cut rim

DATE: 2006

PHOTO: Tim Spriddell

'There are laws and regulations you must comply with (notably HM Revenue and Customs), and a myriad of other things which will all take time away from the actual creative process. Get a good accountant. It is money well saved in the long run.

'Become a member of a professional organisation like Design Factory. It gives great support and puts you in touch with other designer-makers, which can be excellent for advice, collaborations and making good friends. In the same vein, keep in touch with what is happening at the Arts Council and other craft organisations.

Before going self-employed, try working for someone else in the same field for a reasonable amount of time. It is useful to see how it is, or isn't, done well. You are then still learning and being paid for it!

'And finally, enjoy yourself! I am so lucky to have this as my life and earn a living from it.'

This relatively new designer is making work which has different depths of fascination. The patterns on the work are reminiscent of the marks you see in ice that cover the surfaces of ponds in winter.

From surface pattern through mark-making with glass to questions about the function of the piece, Heather Gillespie's glass pieces will evidently be among the collectables of the future. After graduation in 2006, Heather lived for a year in the village of Kamenický Šenov in the Czech Republic, where she spent time refining her craft with Bohemian craftsman skilled in the art of wheel-engraved glass. Then in 2007, with guidance and assistance from the Crafts Council's Next Move Scheme, she started up her own studio. This was based in the glass department at the University of Wolverhampton, but in 2009 she moved to Cumbria, enabling her to produce larger pieces through the neighbouring historical glass company Cumbria Crystal.

Heather combines form with surface pattern created by deep and chiselled cuts made with the diamond, stone and copper wheels that slowly grind away the surface of the glass. The patterns are reminiscent of the marks you see in ice that covers the surface of ponds in winter. This 'frozen memory' approach is a fluid aspect of all of her pieces – vessels, vases, sculptures and lighting.

Heather is fascinated by the extreme states through which glass passes as it is formed and fixed – the molten glass glowing with such intensity of heat and 'behaving like liquid honey', as she puts it, before cooling to its a 'frozen' finished state. 'Seeing molten glass glowing with shades of red, yellow and orange during the heating process, as it swirls in a large pot in the glass furnace, intrigues me. As the work is blown, it changes shape and structure, and once it starts to cool it becomes fixed, as if it were trapped in time. The piece is then transferred to a kiln called a "lehr". After twelve hours of cooling, the piece is ready to handle.'

There are only a few remaining copper-wheel engravers in the UK, and Heather is passionate about preserving traditional techniques through showcasing to new audiences the contemporary results that can be achieved with these age-old processes.

Inspiration comes from what she calls the 'drama of ice and fire and the appeal of the volcanic abundance of Iceland'. But beyond that initial idea lies a lot of work. 'Before creating a piece of glass, I produce a series of sketches and designs. Once the glass has been blown, I begin the process of cutting and polishing it to a high standard, ready for engraving. 'With hand-engraving, each item is a one-off due to the nature of the process. Her techniques are then replicated to produce families and small collections, each following her aesthetics for retaining evidence that each piece is made by hand.

'As I get further into my practice I am starting to produce small batches of vases which are very similar in design whilst offering different sizes – small, medium and large. With these I make to order, leaning upon the skills I have learnt through the making of the individual pieces.'

Heather's work includes pendants of glass detailing aspects of her time in the Czech Republic. Each light is a hand-blown bespoke piece, the colour of which is selected by the client before it is engraved and polished

Her work sells to a number of galleries including both Vessel and Liberty in London.

Right
TITLE: Break the Pattern
lighting (detail)
DATE: 2008
PHOTO: Tas Kyprianou

The signature collection of Rothschild & Bickers comprises a series of glass pendants which pay homage to their sources of inspiration.

Victoria Rothschild and Mark Bickers both studied a BA in Craft and met whilst studying for an MA at the Royal College of Art. In 2003 they started to design work under their own names and to collaborate on a new collection of works that was unveiled in 2006 at the 100% Design exhibition in London. The partnership sourced funding through NESTA (see the list of contacts at the end of the book), and they also received invaluable advice on planning the business, being encouraged to see this as a creative challenge as great as designing the products themselves.

Each piece is made by hand at their glass studio in east London. The studio is one of a few still remaining in the UK which continues to promote the craftsmanship behind the production of blown glass.

Each piece is worked upon by both Mark and Victoria throughout its gestation: from the heat and drama of the hot workshop, through the cold-working processes to ultimately packing up the piece for dispatch. The duo also design together, using their different experiences to influence new work.

What is striking about their collections is their timeless quality. Inspired by historical periods such as the Victorian era, in which decoration and elaborate trimmings were raised to the same level of importance as function, Rothschild & Bickers lean upon heritage without compromising lighting

Right

The workshop and tools of
Victoria and Mark
PHOTO: Rothschild and
Bickers Photography

design solutions for the 21st-century contexts presented to them by their clients.

Their signature collection comprises a series of glass pendants which pay homage to their sources of inspiration. Shades such as the Tassel Light draw design ideas and accents from Victorian decadence, using the trademark combining of materials with which the design practice has become synonymous. The smooth, almost clinical surface and the deep colours of the glass marry beautifully with the fringe of a gold textile tassel frill, which by contrast seems particularly elaborate.

'We strive to promote handmade glass by combining traditional techniques with contemporary design. By blending these elements we hope that our lights sit equally well in both modern and period interiors,' explains Mark.

Not surprisingly, the duo think very carefully about all aspects of their designs, such as the use of colour. 'Colour is a very important element when

working with glass as it transmits and refracts light so well. Our palette was very carefully chosen to evoke classic grandeur whilst not being garish. We were mindful that we wanted all our ranges to sit well with each other.'

Rothschild & Bickers also work in a design-consultancy capacity, creating bespoke pieces for individual clients. Lighting has been designed for the fashion retailer Ted Baker in the UK, Ireland and most recently Australia, whilst designs have also been created for a number of high-end restaurants and for some of the most design-conscious bars such as the famous Yellow House Bar and Restaurant in Rathfarnham, Dublin.

'We think that our main strength as designer-makers is our understanding of glass as a material,' says Victoria. 'We can design a proposal for a specific location, taking advantage of what we know is technically possible whilst still pushing the boundaries of the process. This means we can offer a complete package for interior designers, from concept to resolution.'

She adds, 'My advice for emerging designers would be to organise the logistics of making your products before promoting any of your designs, and also to have a business plan and a goal.

'Don't be afraid to delegate work and tap into other people's skills. You can't do everything and make sure you pay yourself! If you are not making a profit then you are not in business, it is just a hobby.'

Above (A & B)
TITLE: Opulent Optic
MATERIAL: Hand-blown glass
DATE: 2007
Above (C)
TITLE: Tassel Light – Ruby
MATERIAL: Hand-blown glass
DATE: 2007
Above (D)
TITLE: Vintage Light
MATERIAL: Hand-blown glass
DATE: 2007
PHOTOS: All by Simon Camper

Left (E)
TITLE: Spindle Shade
MATERIAL: Hand-blown glass
DATE: 2008
PHOTO: Simon Camper

It is incredibly rare that a designer-maker can be equally as competent in working with two materials, especially when their properties and processes in production require different skills.

Simon Moore is a British ceramicist and glass-maker. University courses still offer multidisciplinary courses yet surprisingly craft makers tend to specialise in just one expressive medium.

The common denominator, however, between glass and ceramics is that the craftsman is required to have an understanding for form, colour, texture and tactility, all of which are properties synonomous with the work of Simon Moore.

Simon was introduced to ceramics at the age of 12 when he visited a pottery in the Hebrides, Scotland. He describes the pottery as a 'basic studio, with two people throwing and a large gas kiln. All the work was run-of-the-mill production brown pottery, but its process fascinated me. I would stand for hours watching them throw, totally mesmerized by the sight of the gas kiln in reduction.'

Simon's work is a beautiful fusion of form, function and colour. He creates pieces of work which show a level of perfection and skill which has evidently been increasing in momentum as he celebrates two decades of British Design and Craft.

His first exhibition was in 1984 at the Marlborough House Gallery. Simon recalls, 'It was a provincial gallery that had a good reputation and was the first show of one-off objects of my work, which consisted of mostly plates and bowls.'

Today his studio (in which he designs) is based in Bideford in Devon, where he also has his workshop (in which he makes). Initially Simon created all of his own works, but for a time he had a small team of four craftspeople who assisted in the creation and completion of his pieces. Now he has returned to working on his own with one assistant, and whilst batch production is part of the work he is re-focusing his own work on larger-scale cast-glass objects.

Simon has an illustrious background, which has made him into the designer of glass and ceramics that he is today. He was design director for Dartington Crystal for three and a half years and he also gained experience of the material whilst being the Creative Director of Salviati, and manager of the small factory on the island of Murano in Venice, which is famous for world-class glass.

Simon is passionate about preserving traditional skills for the next generation of designers and makers. He not only produces his own works, but also teaches courses where knowledge can be transferred and shared, explored and challenged.

'The UK has such a poor manufacturing base, that so many of the traditions of handmade skills have been lost. The crafts world has been chasing the accolades of the art world, thinking that the concept is all important, but in actual fact it is both the idea and the skill that makes it. In doing so the crafts world has colluded in the lack of respect for the handmade'.

'Craft is not just about objects in galleries – it's about ship build, and beautifully restored sash window frames. It is a discipline, and requires to be taught in such a way. It's been too easy for art schools to teach and push the conceptual side of the work and not the real nitty-gritty of how you make your good idea.'

Reminding us of the craftsmanship behind an object is coherent within Simon's portfolio. Being educated within traditional values has taught him to lean upon the past whilst feeding his imagination to create his centrepieces, which are beautifully balanced with contemporary aesthetics.

Today Moore's work is colourful and brash, sensitive and tactile. His lighting and chandeliers show extravagance and imagination exploding through contemporary forms, yet at the heart of their success lies Simon's past experience of working on restoration projects and in repairing treasured luminaries.

His works sell in galleries and retail outlets worldwide, including Harrods and the boutique gallery and visionary gallery Vessel, London (see the Behind the Scenes section of the book to meet the owners). He exhibits at trade fairs such as Maison et Objet in Paris (a twice-yearly trade fair which attracts European and international retail buyers) and ICFF (The International Contemporary Furniture Fair in New York).

His advice for the next generation of designer makers is to 'Learn your craft, but do not expect to be taught. It is up to you to learn, and that takes time.'

Opposite
TITLE: Orange Collection
MATERIAL: Coloured lead crystal.
DATE: 2008
PHOTO: John Russell

Above
TITLE: Stone-finished vases
MATERIAL: Hand-blown lead crystal, surface-cut by diamond wheel
DATE: 2009
PHOTO: John Russell

Left
TITLE: 'Wave' in olive series, blown dishes shaped by hand
MATERIAL: Coloured lead crystal
DATE: 2008
PHOTO: Courtesy of the artist

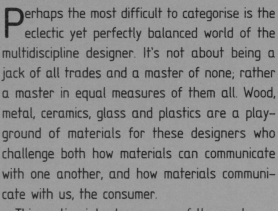

Multidisciplinary

Perhaps the most difficult to categorise is the eclectic yet perfectly balanced world of the multidiscipline designer. It's not about being a jack of all trades and a master of none; rather a master in equal measures of them all. Wood, metal, ceramics, glass and plastics are a playground of materials for these designers who challenge both how materials can communicate with one another, and how materials communicate with us, the consumer.

This section introduces some of the most successful designers and makers who construct and deconstruct our relationships with products and craft. They invite us into their experiments and science labs of design through the outcomes they produce, offering solutions to everyday problems whilst passing comments which make you take life less seriously.

The multidiscipline designer pushes together craft with advances in technology which transform inventions from the pages of a sketchbook into well-executed products. Some of these 'one off' outcomes pay homage to the concepts themselves, whilst others are met with mass market manufacture for design-led consumption.

The interaction between final product and environmental impact is often a starting block rather than stumbling block for their designs. Ecological solutions for seating, lighting and jewellery are as diverse as their marriage of materials.

These designers thrive upon human interaction whilst consciously playing with our emotions, life's clichés and our habitats.

Take these designers seriously but be excused for smiling. They are a breed of designers which demand and deserve attention.

Opposite

ARTIST: Benjamin Hubert

TITLE: Heavy Lights

MATERIAL: Thin walled cast concrete

DATE: 2008

PHOTO: Star Photographers

Trying to categorise Alissia is difficult. She has an affinity with materials but also works with machine manufacturing in the production of her cutting-edge collections.

Alissia Melka-Teichroew is a designer based in Brooklyn, New York. She produces thought-provoking and intelligent objects for wearing and for living. Her work sells in the Museum of Modern Art in the USA and also in the Victoria and Albert Museum in the UK and has attracted attention from those keen to manufacture design-led objects whilst trying to bridge materials and craft processes.

'I like my products to have a certain simplicity, but simplicity is a complex thing to achieve. This is why the story behind a product is the key factor. The concept behind my products is to tell a story with a simple object. This object has to embody many things without it cluttering the viewer's thought.'

Trying to categorise Alissia is difficult. She has an affinity with materials but also works with machine manufacturing in the production of her cutting-edge collections.

As she puts it, 'I did make my pieces myself first. After that I played around with materials when I had the opportunity to work in a studio set up for that particular material. I mostly work on paper, computer, in my head, then often prototype things in cardboard or paper as rough ideas.'

Her work includes the use of many different materials and her outcomes are varied. The work is grouped under different thematic headings – Wear, Live, Eat, Electric and Packaging – reflecting the wide range of her activity and experience, as well as the nature of her motivation. 'I learned all mediums to equal measures whilst at university, which included glass, ceramics and jewellery-making. Material never really was the reason for a product – the material came after the concept of the design.'

Her Ring A Day collection (one ring for every day of the week) comprises silhouettes of seven rings which have been chemically etched out of sheets of sterling silver or stainless steel. 'Simply pop a pre-cut ring out of the sheet, polish rough edges with the hand file included, and voilà! The full sheet or individual sheets can become wall art once all the rings have been removed, and may even be worn as a necklace. Just attach a chain to the piece.'

In creating a 'kit' for the everyday jewellery buyer, Alissia is offering a life cycle of interactivity, from design to manufacture. Her work is not hiding processes but celebrating them by engaging the end user in their final stages. Is this flat-pack jewellery or a way of inviting the masses to become makers?

Her Diamond and Pearl Acrylic Rings show us that value is in the eyes of the beholder, as with this jewellery the priceless qualities are not in the material but in the notion of the giving of the ring and the symbolism the ring holds. 'Metals have been deemed "precious" because they're relatively rare, they're shiny, and they last. We value diamonds because they're even rarer, shinier, and durable (and often fraught with human rights concerns). No wonder they are so expensive. Do we really need one to prove our love?' she asks.

Alissia uses laser-cutting techniques, textile-

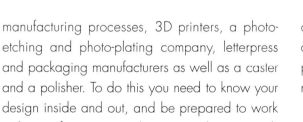

manufacturing processes, 3D printers, a photo-etching and photo-plating company, letterpress and packaging manufacturers as well as a caster and a polisher. To do this you need to know your design inside and out, and be prepared to work with manufacturers to achieve something special. This is exactly what Alissia has succeeded in doing.

This designer challenges our perception of design and materials whilst reminding us that life itself is precious and that maybe sometimes we take it all too seriously. Alissia ought to be celebrated as a visionary of modern times and a designer for modern values, though her own

assessment of the need to be groundbreaking is admirably level-headed. 'Sometimes I do have to push the boundaries for the manufacturing, but it is not always something you set out to do,' she says.

Her advice for new designers is, 'Learn to work with criticism – even if you do not agree, listen to what people have to say. If you don't agree, then try to explain to yourself why not.

'Learn how to speak about design and express your thoughts. Follow your gut instinct but try to understand why you make the choices you make. Choices are what make you the unique designer you are. Find your own "handwriting", your own way, your path, your goal.'

Above

TITLE: The Inside Out collection
MATERIAL: Handblown borosilicate glass
DATE: 2003
PHOTO: Lisa Klappe

Left

TITLE: Cl'e USB.
MATERIAL: Resin and USB device.
DATE: 2008
PHOTO: Jan Habraken

Opposite page

TITLE: Diamond and Pearl Acrylic Rings
MATERIAL: Acrylic
DATE: 2003

Benjamin Hubert graduated from Loughborough University in 2006 and exhibited at the New Designers exhibition at the Business Design Centre in London in the same year.

The following year he launched his studio and collections at the 100% Futures exhibition as part of the London Design Festival. There is something about Benjamin which makes you want to revisit his business start-up date: for someone so young in the design world, Benjamin has created a lot of waves. His timeless designs show an appreciation for interior and space, and his products are manufactured to a high standard through collaborative projects with manufacturers.

A 'materials empathiser' is perhaps a better description for this creative entity rather than the 'industrial designer' that is his preferred title. Materials such as concrete and glass do not become an easy substrate to design with unless the designer first understands their limitations. It is not so easy using these materials to convert designs on a computer into real pieces that work well.

'I get inspiration from a lot of sources. Working closely with materials and process seems to inform my work most. Getting hands-on with things kick-starts my passion for creating new pieces. I really enjoy visiting factories for this reason, but inspira-

tion can come from a range of sources – it might be an article on a blog or an interesting location when travelling. I make some of the prototype pieces, whether they are masters for casting or one-off pieces of furniture. I usually outsource the manufacture if it is outside my skill set.'

Benjamin's projects are manufactured all over the world, and he is obviously drawn to those countries with a specialised industrial tradition in a particular material. 'I have concrete cast in Germany, furniture made in Scandinavia or Eastern Europe, and some things are done in the Far East. The location of manufacture is based on the company I am designing the piece for, the cost, and the skills that are needed.'

It can be said that his work can create a rather unsettling feeling which in normal circumstances would beg one to question his material choices, yet they perform their function incredibly well and showcase his talent for selecting such innovative substrates to work with.

In his glass stemware range entitled Botanical, Benjamin has developed a mouth-blown and hand-

worked martini glass, designed for the Bombay Sapphire gin brand and manufactured by the parent company Bacardi. It consists of a cocktail glass bowl and conventional stem, from the lower end of which various glass strands spread out like the roots of a plant. Structurally, the roots take the place of a conventional base.

Other examples of this experimental way of using materials can be found in his lighting collection entitled Heavy Lights (see p.63), which are thin-walled, cast-concrete lamps – heavy and yet light at the same time, in both material and concept.

His advice for the next generation of designers is, 'Get involved with awards. Go to parties and network.'

'Be patient, it takes a long time to establish yourself. You will get a lot more no's than yes's – you will need to be quite tough.

'Exhibit your work – it's the best way to raise your profile for press and publication.'

Opposite page
TITLE: Diamond Chair
MATERIAL: Tweed, steel and ply veneer
DATE: 2008
PHOTO: Star Photographers

Below
TITLE: Lilly Pad Table
MATERIAL: Solid wood, CNC formed steel
DATE: 2008
PHOTO: Star Photographers

Above
TITLE: Yumbrella Fruit Bowl with Banana Tree
MATERIAL: Earthenware ceramic
DATE: 2008
PHOTO: Star Photographers

Design Glut

DESIGNERS: CREATING A SMILE THROUGH DESIGN (WITH A LITTLE HELP FROM GOOGLE!)

USA

Design Glut is a design partnership between Kegan Fisher and Liz Kinnmark; as a company it has charm, charisma and an ability to make a statement through design.

Based in Brooklyn, New York, Kegan and Liz both graduated from the Pratt Institute in the same city, where they studied industrial design. After graduation, they went into business creating objects that draw upon current events and politics, traditional notions of value, and humour. The collection was unveiled at the International Contemporary Furniture Fair (ICFF) on the Designboom mart stand.

In 2007, the duo created a series entitled Crude. At a time when the news was full of headlines about the ever-increasing cost of oil, they were making jewellery with miniature oil-barrel pendants, pointing out that oil is the new luxury. The Crude collection is an example of what the pair refer to as 'satirical bling'. Each piece has a miniature oil-barrel pendant, engraved with the date it was made and the price of a barrel of oil on that day.

The Design Glut collections include both mass-produced items and those produced on a small scale. The first item they designed that needed a manufacturer to meet demand was their eggcup holder entitled Egg Pants. With no previous knowledge or understanding of how to do this, they did what most people of this generation can now do, and Googled the problem.

'I Googled for dip-moulders, started making phone calls, and sent off a slew of emails with my computer model,' says Liz. 'One factory got back to me with a $500 quote to make the prototype. I, like any college student, was scared out of my mind by the $500 price tag. But again, my teacher encouraged me to do it, and it has turned out to be the best $500 I ever spent.'

When Liz was pleased with the final product she placed it onto the internet, with images of the prototype and a description of the collection. Within one week she had received an email from MOMA (Museum of Modern Art) in New York for a sample, and she now sells the product through their museum shop and online store.

Design Glut's intention is to provoke and excite you with their objects. 'We don't make things unless we truly believe there is a reason for them to exist.' explains Liz. 'Our objects start conversations, cause you to crack a smile and add something meaningful to your life.'

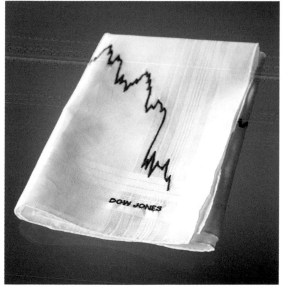

Opposite
TITLE: Hookmaker
MATERIAL: Earthenware clay
DATE: 2007
PHOTO: Design Glut

Their advice for the next generation of designers is, 'Think big and shoot for what you really want, even though it may seem impossibly out of reach at the time.

'Having a brilliant idea is not enough. All of the real work happens in-between having an idea and making it a reality. A sketch of a product is so, so far away from having a product that is manufactured, costed out, packaged and ready to sell.

'Put yourself out there on the internet. So many things are made possible by the internet. Blogs can spread word of your projects around the globe, to stores and press and customers. It is suddenly possible for a little studio in Brooklyn to manufacture things in Thailand, have them published in a Ukrainian magazine and sell them in London. It's amazing! I don't know how anyone started a business 20 years ago.

'It really is who you know, many times. Conversations lead to so many things that you would never expect. Make friends as you go. And finally, have fun. If you don't love what you're doing, this really isn't the easiest way to make a buck. Go do something else.'

Above left
TITLE: Egg Pants
MATERIAL: PVC
DATE: 2006
PHOTO: Beatrice Peltre

Left
TITLE: Dow Jones Hanky
MATERIAL: Linen
DATE: 2009
PHOTO: Design Glut

Above
TITLE: Crude Necklace
MATERIAL: Powder coated brass
DATE: 2007
PHOTO: Design Glut

Molo's inspiration comes from celebrating the simple pleasures life has to offer: shelter, food and love.

Molo is a design studio based in Vancouver in Canada, exploring how a product interacts with a space, and how its appearance relates to its function. You cannot help but feel that their designs emerge from a laboratory of investigations, interactions and experiments, but also, most importantly, a sense of playfulness. Todd MacAllen and Stephanie Forsythe, molo's founders, have a varied background of study including sciences, fine arts and architecture. However, as Todd explains, 'our attitude in the studio is that we are still all students'.

Todd refers to himself as 'designer, architect, entrepreneur, merchant, quality-control monitor, janitor and even maintenance guy', highlighting that the success of this practice is their hands-on approach and their passion for problem-solving through design, whilst keeping their feet on the ground.

'In the beginning we made almost everything ourselves. Then we began to subcontract some of the work to specialists. More and more of the production is being subcontracted, but we always develop and make the prototypes in-studio. We believe quite strongly in the idea that the hands play an important role in the design process – we design with our hands.'

Molo forms marriages with manufacturers, but they explain that it is not an easy process. 'Most of our production is now done by specialists who we have developed a "partnership" with. We work with craftspeople around the world that have a unique ability and the desire to work with us.'

Their products combine subtle and elegant forms with a conscious approach to how a space can be altered using temporary structures. Their 'soft' series, for instance, has been created to 'redefine and open spaces' using structures which concertina – stretching and retracting – to create intimate hybrid environments and soften hard-edged interiors.

In 2004 molo was awarded the New Designers award at the ICFF, held at the Javitz Centre in New York, and in 2006 'soft' was purchased by the Museum of Modern Art in New York for their permanent collection.

The drinking vessel collection, 'float', is another example of how they are able to produce beautiful design through play. Leaning upon its designers'

Right
TITLE: 'Float', small tea lantern with sugar and cream
MATERIAL: Cylinders of German glass
DATE: 2004
PHOTO: Courtesy of molo

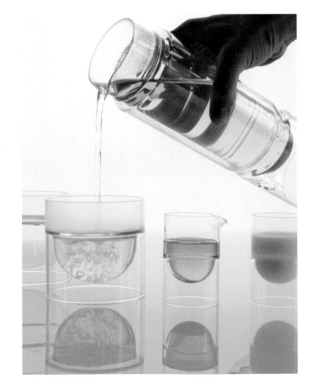

scientific background, this clinical yet timeless collection is produced using thermally resistant glass which creates an insulated space between the user and the beverage.

Molo's inspiration comes from celebrating the simple pleasures life has to offer: shelter, love and food. Their world is one where the pace of life becomes much slower and calmer. If you rush by, you risk missing work which deserves to be among the design icons of the future.

Todd and Stephanie's top tips for emerging designers are, 'Do it for your own delight and satisfaction. Work persistently and work hard.

'If you have your own business it is always a part of you and you need to be OK with this. You can't take a vacation from it – it comes with you!

'Rely on your intuition but think over your decisions carefully and frugally.

'And finally, share your work with others – show the world what you are doing.'

Left
TITLE: 'Soft' seating
MATERIAL: Kraft paper
DATE: 2006
PHOTO: Courtesy of molo.

Autoban draws inspiration from how people use a product and also where the product will live in the home or interior space.

Seyhan Özdemir and Sefer Çaglar are the designers behind the Turkish design company Autoban which was established in 2003. Since this time the practice has grown from being two designers to employing thirty people. Their fresh and uncompromising approach to designing tables, chairs, lighting and beds has made this practice one of the most prominent young voices in international furniture design. They are also Istanbul's most sought after, with their ability to create products and interior spaces which embrace modern Turkish lifestyles. Autoban are not only designing products for interiors but also creating interiors for products.

In 2005, they were selected by style magazine *Wallpaper* as one of the top five young designers in the world, and in the same year they won Best Newcomer at the 100% Design exhibition in London.

Seyhan explains their development and overall philosophy. 'We started with designing interiors for cafés, restaurants and residential spaces, and we always consider all furniture and space as part of a whole concept. We enjoy both interior design and product as well, but feel more free while designing products.'

The craftsmanship behind their pieces demonstrates an appreciation for the intrinsic qualities of the materials they use. They draw inspiration from how people use a product and also where the product will live in the home or interior space. The function of the product seems to be at the centre of their problem-solving in the creation of statement pieces of furniture for interiors.

Based in Istanbul, their design practice has grown considerably within the interior design sector. As you approach the Autoban design studio you are faced with ornate arches and vast imposing wooden doors, reminiscent of times gone by in Turkish architecture. In contrast, the space inside now houses 20 or more creative practitioners all of which work alongside Seyhan and Sefer on interior projects. The products themselves however, still originate from Seyhans and Sefers passion for

This page
TITLE: Double Octopus
MATERIAL: Aluminium rods
and light bulbs
DATE: 2005
PHOTO: Autoban/
De La Espada

industrial processes whilst being inspired by every-day rituals, daily lifestyles and nature.

In their chair which they call 'Nest', Autoban have created a personal habitat enclosure for escapism reminiscent of a child's cot. Autoban are a sponge for the dynamic and design-hungry city they are based in, yet there is a sophisticated balance in their products which draws upon the heritage of their country and delivers answers for modern times.

Seyhan explains; 'We like thinking back to memories of a particular lifestyle or atmosphere and drawing inspiration from that.'

With products such as Wired King, a wire frame freestanding light inspired by traditional Turkish forms and the sidetable-come-stool design Ottoman, it is clear that the language of a country, its heart beat and its soul are being preserved through mod-ernist design.

Seyhan and Sefer's advice for the next genera-tion of designers is, 'First find your own individual style and approach, and find ways to be original. Travel far and read many books.

'Be "in the kitchen", which means deal with all works related to design – both small (seems unim-portant) and very important ones.'

And finally, 'designate people's roles appropriately when your business grows. Motivate people and give them a purpose and a passion for what they do.'

Far left
TITLE: The studio and
showroom
PHOTO: Courtesy of
Autoban

Left
TITLE: Nest chair
MATERIAL: Wood
DATE: 2009
PHOTO: Mustafa Nurdogdu

Chris Kabel is a multidiscipline and multitalented designer, working with materials whilst playing with nostalgia. He designs work which makes you ask yourself, 'Why has nobody else thought of that?'.

Somehow, Chris still finds time to be quirky, fun and experimental, with an aesthetic geared toward usage, which he calls his main inspiration. He works from a studio in Rotterdam, where he moved in 2002, on project briefs for clients and on his own in-house design collections.

Chris has had a design journey which is typical of many other designer-makers. He is inquisitive and wants to know how things work. 'I took apart my mother's antique clock at the age of nine,' explains Chris. 'When my mother got angry with me for destroying the thing I tried to put it back together. Although it didn't look at all like before, it worked. It was more beautiful than any other clock I had ever seen. It has remained unchanged since then and it still works.'

Chris is a magpie for materials, collecting and hoarding information that he comes by on his travels to other countries and through life. He calls himself a 'surgeon', and one can imagine him with his scalpel taking apart a product that calls for some tinkering and changing it into something completely new.

In 2003 he was nominated for the Rotterdam Design Prize for a chandelier he designed using symmetrical elements which could be joined onto one another to create larger installations, and in 2006 he was awarded the Red Dot Design Award for a tablecloth called Tableshapes. In 2009 he was awarded the Dutch Material Prize for his innovative use of material in his Seam Chair.

Kabel likes to engage and challenge his audience. He strives to encourage a reaction within all of his pieces. In 2005 he designed a napkin called 2fold, which encouraged the diner to create origami with their napkin whilst waiting for their food to be served.

It is fair to say that the eccentricities behind some of his work are reminiscent of a scrap-heap challenge. A marriage between different components that normally would not be associated with one another enabled the designer to create something new. Chris is leaning upon his empathy for craft and yet blurring boundaries with personal memories, whilst romancing the end consumer with his playful designs and products.

Flames was the title of a 'refillable gas-fuelled candelabra' (see p.1) a design that grew out of a camping gas bottle. Later this was followed by a design for a chandelier, again using the gas bottle at the core of the design with pipes which stemmed from the canister to provide gas to the arms of the chandelier.

Parasols made from green-lace leaves which create shade like a tree canopy, vases with holes in, silicon-lace tablecloths, a vase made from money, sticky lamps and chocolate clocks – all embrace Kabel's aesthetic of good design and off-the-wall humour.

Chris is associated with two main design houses in the Netherlands – Droog Design and Mooi – which help in sourcing manufacturing for his collections and in spreading the word for the work he creates at home and abroad.

Chris's advice for new designers is, 'You need to be determined, stubborn, slightly naive, very positive and highly energetic to start for yourself. But in the end there's no fixed recipe for success – you have to find your own way.'

Opposite
TITLE: Sticky Lamp
MATERIAL: PET lamp fitting
DATE: 2001
PHOTO: Courtesy of the artist

Below
TITLE: Shady Lace
MATERIAL: Weatherproof lace
DATE: 2003
PHOTO: Courtesy of the artist

Top
TITLE: Flotsam Vase
MATERIAL: Rotational moulded vase in recycled LDPE – limited edition by Plust Italy
DATE: 2009
PHOTO: Courtesy of the artist

Above
TITLE: Seam Chair
MATERIAL: Polypropylene
DATE: 2007
PHOTO: Courtesy of the artist

Michael Marriott studied at the London College of Furniture in 1985, which he describes as a 'really good, old-school trade school with essentially technical training'.

In 1999 Michael won the Jerwood Furniture Prize. What is clear when you begin to look at Michael's work is this early planting of a 'hands-on and technical education', which prepared him for being the inventor and explorer of materials that he is today.

Michael is a great communicator through design – he not only empathises with the material but looks at the existence of objects and our need to surround ourselves with them.

His interest in education and the importance this holds for the next generation of designers has led him to teach at the Royal College of Art since completing his MA at the same institution.

Based in London, Michael has set up his studio perfectly to fulfil the fuctions he requires from a work space: a place where he is able to create working prototypes and translate designs quickly, but perhaps most importantly somewhere he can live with an idea before finalising the design.

Michael has collaborated on a number of projects and continues to grow his reputation for creating marriages between craft and design by working with companies such as Trico in Tokyo, Inflate, SCP, and most recently with the British company Established & Sons.

Not scared of new challenges, in 2009 Michael was invited to explore new relationships between man and machine. The project was instigated by Metropolitan Works, who invited nine leading figures to explore and develop new works using their £4.5 million facility (see the list of helpful contacts for details about Metworks). Michael created the Sunsum Stool, which was inspired by the traditional Ashanti stools from Ghana in West Africa. This investigative body of work was created using state-of-the-art digital manufacturing technology.

Michael is inspired by function and by how the item may be reproduced. He explains, 'I am very interested in material and process, but also in how people use objects. I am intrigued by how the object, design or function may inform the natural outcome of a product beyond its aesthetics.'

There seems to be a story behind all of his works. With this story you find a question, whilst the end product becomes the answer. Michael looks for problems to solve and finds the solution for making design become great design.

His advice for the next generation of designers is, 'Be yourself, be committed, be passionate, work hard and enjoy what you do.'

Opposite
TITLE: Hereford Chair
MATERIAL: Solid ash
DATE: 2008
PHOTO: Lisa Linder

Below
TITLE: Readymade, Recycled
MATERIAL: Beech kitchen
stool, bicycle forks, electric
components
DATE: 2006
PHOTO: Briony Campbell

Right
TITLE: Tico XL 1.2
MATERIAL: Tamo, birch
plywood and steel bar
DATE: 2006
PHOTO: Hitoshi Saeki

Below right
TITLE: Looking Bench
MATERIAL: Solid oak, steel
bar
DATE: 2008
PHOTO: Ivan Sutherland

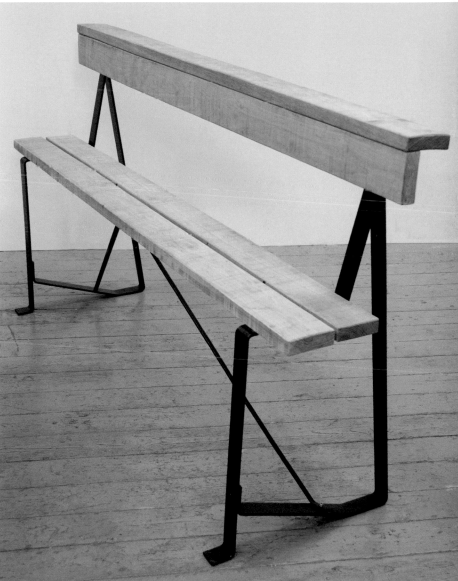

MICHAEL MARRIOTT

Textiles

This chapter showcases some of the most pro-lific designers and makers fusing textile craft with design. As with ceramics and glass, the textile industry in Europe has been in rapid decline over the last few decades. In the UK, regions such as Nottinghamshire, Leicestershire and Yorkshire once boasted mills and manufacturing houses across the landscape; nowadays few school leavers would re-alise that these cities were once famous for tex-tiles, garments and knitwear production.

In recent years however, there has a been a strong revival through craft and design, with mak-ers collaborating with some of the remaining mills in the production of new works and the develop-ment of new approaches. Textiles are moving back into the home with a quirky attitude which brings together traditional craft and modern ideals.

Knitting in particular has seen a great revival over the last ten years, with textile designers rein-venting knitted products for the home, spurring on a nation of DIY fanatics to dig out their grand-mothers' needles and teach themselves how to 'knit one, purl one'. Knitting was once a common pastime associated mainly with the likes of the Women's In-stitute. However, just as the WI is changing (open-ing a branch at Goldsmiths University in London in 2009 – the first student-based WI in the Institute's history) so too are people's ideas for keeping tra-ditions alive. Clubs such as Stitch and Bitch, estab-lished in 2005 in London, are embracing our home-grown and home-produced memories and engaging new generations to meet, engage in conversation and share knitting techniques over a glass of wine.

This new appetite for everything stitched, sewn and knitted owes a tremendous debt to the de-signers and makers who have successfully placed textiles as a craft into the designer marketplace, creating current trends, and ensuring textiles are being pushed into new territories whilst embracing technology, sustainability and traditional values.

Opposite

TITLE: Rosette Wall Panel
ARTIST: Anne Kyrrö Quinn
MATERIAL: Wool felt
DATE: 2007
PHOTO: 7 Gods London

Anne Kyyrö Quinn's work is designed to attract attention and provoke the senses. It is impossible simply to look at the work she produces – you need to touch, feel and live with these creations.

From cushions and throws to sculptural wall panels in bold colours, textiles have played an integral role in Anne's life. 'Since I was a child I have been interested in textile handicrafts. We also have a long tradition in textile design and art in my native Finland.'

When asked to talk about her inspiration, Anne says, 'Inspiration is everywhere – even the materials I work with are inspiring'. It is clear that Anne loves the experimentation and the challenge of making textiles feel three-dimensional without stripping an object of its function.

Experimentation with materials and how a fabric can be folded and joined together is important to Anne. 'I am inspired by the structure of the fabric and how the textile can be used structurally. It has been very interesting working with architectural installations, and I have discovered how my ideas and techniques can be used on larger scales. It has also been interesting to discover how important textiles are acoustically within interiors, which has been overlooked in modern interior design.'

Folds, twists, curves and pleats all add depth and intrigue to Anne's surface patterning, whilst her challenging use of materials adds new dimensions to functional design.

In 2001, her Cable Floor Lamp won *Light* magazine's Best of Show at the Lighting Show at the NEC in Birmingham in England, and was the first product to use pleated felt in a lampshade. Other accolades include Best New Designer at the ICFF exhibition in New York, and in 2009 Anne was awarded the good design award by the Chicago Anthenaeum.

Her career started life in the same way as those of many other designer-makers in recent times. In July 1998, straight out of university, she exhibited at the New Designers show at the Business Design Centre in Islington, launched her work the following year and then continued to show through exhibitions.

At this time Anne was making all the work herself from her home. When demand increased she sourced the making of the textiles she designed, such as the cushions and throws, in multiples. It was important to her that this extended arm of production was kept in the UK, and to that end she researched small textile workshops in Yorkshire (the hub of England's textile industry) and Scotland.

Today she employs a team of makers at her studio, who collaborate in the making of the creations she designs.

In addition to the support from the press, Anne initially sought financial and business support to enable her to reach the platform she has today. 'I received the setting-up grant from the Crafts Council in 2000. Thereafter I have received exhibition bursaries from Design Nation over the years and various grants from UK Trade and Investment, who

have helped me with exhibiting abroad.'

Anne sells her work to design retailers and boutiques, private clients and interior designers worldwide. 'Our customers are mainly interior designers and architects who commission custom-made products for their projects,' she says. 'The products have also grown from cushions and small textile items into wall installations and large acoustic panels and curtains which are almost always tailored to site-specific projects.'

Anne is a strong supporter of using your networking skills to communicate with others. Her advice for a new designer entering the design world would be to, 'Ensure your ideas are original. Have passion and believe in your work and ideas, whilst also working incredibly hard to achieve your ambition.'

Opposite

TITLE: Leaf Wall Panel

MATERIAL: 100% wool felt

DATE: 2007

PHOTO: Courtesy of the artist

Above right

TITLE: Diamond Leaf Wall Panel

MATERIAL: 100% wool felt

installation, London

DATE: 2009

PHOTO: Luzelle van der Westhuizen

Right

TITLE: Green Diagonal Twist panel

MATERIAL: 100% Wool Felt

DATE: 2007

PHOTO: Courtesy of the artist

Based in Boston, Massachusetts, Etcetera Media is a design company specialising in products which use industrial felt to make bags, vessels, interior accessories and children's toys.

The design practice was officially formed in 2006 by designers Kelly Smith and Chris Grimley, partners in both design and marriage. Chris continued his education to graduate with a master's in Architecture from the University of British Columbia in 2000, while Kelly graduated from Northeastern University, Boston in 2003 where she studied architecture.

'After graduation I was working at an architecture office when I started sewing things on the side – mostly bags made out of used clothing,' explains Kelly. 'One of my co-workers asked me to design and make a laptop bag for him, and I came across this gorgeous German felt.'

Felt is a traditional material which has been used for centuries by the farming industries, and is also a common craft material. The difference with Etcetera Media is the way they combine this traditional material, essentially 'recycled from sheep', with cutting-edge forms and challenging functions such as in the 100% wool-felt wine rack.

To Chris the material offers a set of limits to work within, and with their backgrounds in architecture and in understanding structures, the duo find felt to be eminently suited to being manipulated, sewn and folded to create 3D sculptural forms. 'In general, the material is often the inspiration. Finding out how it moves, folds, cuts, can be sewn – and those limitations often push the direction of a product's design.'

Kelly started by making the bags herself but has been able to source local assistance with the sewing of the most mainstream items, though she continues to sew new collections and working samples. The wine racks are still made by hand by the designer herself.

Etcetera Media's work is beautifully executed, and although at first glance it may appear to be produced by mechanical processes, it becomes clear that each and every piece is crafted with the

highest degree of skill. They successfully create functional, architectural and structural craft which needs to be worn and to adorn, but also, most importantly, to be lived with. Their top tips for future designers are:

'Don't be afraid to make the leap. There will be really scary moments where you have no money or no one knows your work, but you have to push through them. That first moment after handing in the letter of resignation at the day job is simultaneously exciting and scared-to-death frightening.

'Collaborate or share ideas with the people around you. You'll be surprised at what other ideas come out of such conversations.

Above

TITLE: 6-Pack Wine Rack

MATERIAL: 3mm ($1/8$ in.) thick wool felt

DATE: 2007

PHOTO: Courtesy of the artist

'Try to (eventually) separate work from home. Try not to live at work or work at home.

'Do more and think less. The less control you give to your brain, the more surprised you will be at the results.

'And finally, push yourself to learn new techniques. Even though you think you have no time, build it into the schedule. Carving time is easier when you plan it.'

Opposite

TITLE: The Northampton Bag – Black

MATERIAL: 3mm ($1/8$ in.) thick wool felt from Danish wool

DATE: 2008

PHOTO: Courtesy of the artist

Below

TITLE: Book Box

MATERIAL: 3mm ($1/8$ in.) thick wool felt from Danish wool

DATE: 2008

PHOTO: Courtesy of the artist

Below

TITLE: Coasters in studio

MATERIAL: Die-cut dual-coloured felt

DATE: 2008

PHOTO: Courtesy of the artist

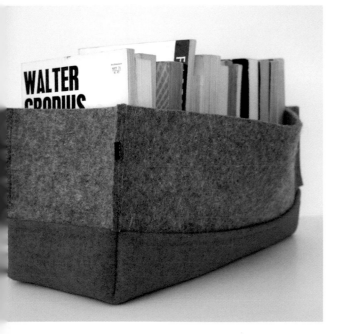

After graduating in Textiles from Chelsea College of Art and completing an MA in Woven Textiles at the RCA, Margo Selby gained a fellowship with The Ann Sutton Foundation.

The Ann Sutton Foundation is an organisation that was formed to raise the profile and design quality of woven textiles. The foundation nurture imaginative design research into the tactile and visual qualities of the new fibres and yarns that are crucial for the continuing vitality of the textile industry.

The Foundation afforded her a secure environment to continue to develop her work, by providing a studio space and a paid means of earning a living. Margo describes it as an 'amazing opportunity'. During this period, she worked collaboratively with two other weavers also in receipt of the fellowship, but also on developing her own personal approach to new projects.

The knowledge of traditional craft and manufacture that she gained through her time with the Sutton Foundation enabled Margo to experiment and push the boundaries of woven textiles. She began designing and making fabrics for couture fashion collections, producing tablecloths for a party at The National Portrait Gallery and developing fabrics for a scarf company on which she would receive royalties for every sale.

Soon Margo began her search for a mill in the

UK that would enable her to collaborate in production, using her inside knowledge of what was possible and how far this could be pushed to achieve original, exciting and luxurious products. After visiting a number of jacquard mills Margo found one in Yorkshire that was not only able to produce her designs, but also offered her freelance design work. (Jacquard is the name given to a loom designed in 1801 by Joseph Marie Jacquard, which is operated by the use of hole-punched cards. The loom is able to create highly decorative and detailed patterns.) 'I had no idea about setting up a business and branding myself at all, although I did give myself a company name, Margo Selby – looming marvellous!'

Through trade fairs and press attention Margo's work began to move into the public domain. It became clear that there was a need for her work, a market for her creations and the potential to create a business.

While working for the weave mills, Margo produced highly commercial designs for interiors and traditional furnishing fabrics. It was the restrictiveness of these briefs, however, that led her to a more innovative approach and a different use of yarns. 'I was completely opportunistic, giving anything a go and treating each project as a learning experience, whether paid or not.'

In the beginning, a lot of work was unpaid, but the experience she gained was worth the hardship. The customer and manufacturing contacts she gained, and the knowledge of how to work towards a professional end result, were invaluable.

Margo calls herself a designer-maker, 'but I am so definitely a craftsperson. Ultimately, first and foremost, I am a weaver'.

In 2003, Margo received a Setting Up Grant from the Crafts Council and launched her new label, Margo Selby. As part of the terms of this grant she was also given support and knowledge in how to run a craft business. In this context, she says, 'When at college or when given advice, it only becomes really relevant when you are actually doing it yourself.'

The year 2007 saw the grand opening of Margo's retail space and studio in the heart of Bloomsbury in London, and in addition to the collections she has created for the design retailer Habitat, her clients now include independent design shops and galleries worldwide.

Margo's advice for the next generation of designers is 'Always stay true to yourself and trust your own instincts about your work. Understand your market and where you fit into this. Know who your customers are and what they will spend on certain products. Look closely at the prices of similar products on the market. Whilst you shouldn't undersell yourself it is important to be realistic about how much people will be prepared to spend on the items you are selling.

'Plan ahead. Business and financial planning are crucial tools for successful business. Cash flow and financial forecasting may seem overwhelming at first but there is great satisfaction in knowing exactly where you are with your business, and this will give you confidence to make successful business decisions. Having a five-year plan will also help you to focus on future goals.

'Be open-minded and versatile about working with people and collaborating. You can move the business forward in exciting ways and gain exposure to new markets by teaming up with other individuals or businesses on collaborative projects. Keep an open mind on how you may work in the future with other businesses.

'And finally, be brave and be prepared to take some risks. These risks can be calculated and backed up with good business planning and financial forecasting.

Opposite
TITLE: Galeano and Paradise Cushions
MATERIAL: 80% silk, 20% lycra
DATE: 2010
PHOTO: Courtesy of the artist

Above
TITLE: Handwoven Scarf
MATERIAL: Cashmere, silk, lambswool
DATE: 2009
PHOTO: Courtesy of the artist

Below
TITLE: Weekender Bags
MATERIAL: Fabric with leather trims
DATE: 2009
PHOTO: Courtesy of the artist

Tait & Style's design aesthetic is simple: to create a range of designs, from rich, comforting, textural woollies to quirky graphic designs that are both elegant and humorous.

Behind the successful textile company Tait & Style, you'll find Ingrid Tait, a designer and maker who is passionate about fusing couture design with traditional processes to create fun, quirky yet luxurious scarves, blankets, cushions and children's toys.

Within a few months of embarking on her career in textiles, whilst still at university, Ingrid was offered a second-hand needle-punching machine that in the long run would prove the answer to manufacturing her work and keeping up with increasing demand. She immediately saw the potential in exploring the machine's possible applications and in creating links between this traditional process of manufacture and how it could lend itself to the world of modern fashion.

'The only problem was where to put this big, cast-iron machine? Back in Orkney, my father had come across part of an old school that the council were starting to rent out. He thought it might be suitable for me, so I came to have a look. It was cheap, spacious, and had a great view in the lovely fishing town of Stromness. So, despite loving London, and having imagined that I would be staying on there for much longer, I moved back to Orkney in 1990.'

Ingrid applied for business start-up assistance from The Highlands and Islands Development Board (HIDB), who provided her with some initial grant aid and the support of business advisers.

Passion for craft and design is a coherent strand in all of Ingrid's work. She is aware of her customer base, and develops collections which attract different audiences, all of whom have in common an appreciation of craft, quality, skill and design.

Tait & Style use a variety of techniques including crochet, felting, hand and machine knitting, whilst fusing fabrics and manipulating weaves and yarns. 'Most of the making is actually done by highly skilled and flexible knitters and sewers here in Orkney, who I've worked with for years. I do make one-off needle-punched pieces myself, but on the whole we work as a team. I also design jewellery (my mother is the pioneering Scottish

Right

TITLE: Pom Bomb Pin
Cushion

DATE: 2002

MATERIAL: 100% lambswool

PHOTO: Marcia Mihotitch

jewellery designer Ola Gorie) and again I work with the best makers I can find to turn my design ideas into reality.'

As with many designers and makers, the needs of starting a company and setting up in business has required Ingrid to become a one-woman band and a master of all trades. She does this exceptionally well, by helping current students on work placements (previous recipients have included the designers Donna Wilson and Alison Willoughby) or collaborating with other designers who create work for the Tait & Style label.

'Our local fish shop has a sign up above its counter: "GOOD FISH ISN'T CHEAP AND CHEAP FISH ISN'T GOOD". I sometimes feel the same could be said about textiles!' Ingrid remarks.

Tait & Style can be found in prestigious retailers in Paris, Tokyo, New York and London who share the empathy for high design and high craftsmanship. The company also has its own boutique on Orkney. In 2010 Ingrid received the Jerwood Contemporary Maker Award.

Ingrid's advice for the next generation of designers is as follows: 'I don't think there is any one big piece of advice, one secret for success for designers (or if there is, I've never found it!). I suppose I have accumulated a lot of knowledge and experience over the years, and in overcoming various obstacles to survival. But I find it easier and more useful to pass that on one-to-one on a case-by-case basis, when working with students or young designers' rather than by straining to come up with generalisations.'

Opposite

TITLE: At work in the studio.

PHOTO: Courtesy of the artist

Right

TITLE: Fetlar

MATERIAL: 100% wool

DATE: 2004

PHOTO: John Paul

Donna Wilson's work is extraordinary: magical, strangely surreal and yet comforting at the same time.

Donna is a creator, an innovator, and is undoubtedly responsible for expanding the possibilities of knitting in the 21st century. Childhood memories of fictional characters come alive through names such as Cyril Squirrel-fox, a knitted crossbreed of a squirrel and a fox who is described as 'mischievous and likes marmalade but dislikes cottage cheese'. Then there is Pierre, a pink-eared and stripey-legged character who 'loves drinking tea and having the odd bit of chocolate but hates wasps'.

These are not just children's toys, but toys for grown-ups who secretly long to escape into the world of make-believe.

Donna calls herself a designer-maker. 'I really like the fact that I manufacture work here. As things have grown, time for designing gets more and more limited, so I have to design when I can, like when I'm sitting on the train or lying in bed at night!'

Inspiration stems from childhood memories and, as she explains, 'the naivety of children's drawings, colour, pattern and form.'

Funding for her business was helped by a Crafts Council Development Award, but Donna admits that the driving force behind her work, as with so many designers, is her own passionate commitment for what she does. 'Nearly all the money I earn gets put back into the company for more products.'

Her work was initially showcased in an exhibition hosted by the Crafts Council called Knit 2 Together, which, as she explains, 'opened up my work to a much greater audience'. Her first solo show was in 2009 at the Lighthouse in Glasgow, where she showed a 20-metre-long scene full of knitted trees and creatures.

When Donna first set up her business after graduating in 2005, she was making all of her creatures herself, but as her success grew she began to source help in the knitting and the assembly of the collections. 'I get lots of my knitting done in Galashiels in Scotland. I am really keen to keep the production all in the UK and handmade. I think it makes them special. I don't want to get them mass-produced.'

Today Donna is expanding her collections with furniture collaborations and accessories that utilise her surface patterns and designs.

Donna's work is sold in shops, boutiques, galleries and department stores worldwide including the Yorkshire Sculpture Park in the UK, Addiction in Hong Kong and Incu in New Zealand. Her advice for new designers is, 'to know your market and where your work fits into the marketplace. Be unique and start small. Believe in yourself and be confident about your product, but most of all enjoy what you do.'

Left
TITLE: Berty the Knitted Bird
MATERIAL: Knitted lambswool
DATE: 2009
PHOTO: Donna Wilson

Right
TITLE: Baby Raccoon (Rill)
MATERIAL: Knitted lambswool creature
DATE: 2008
PHOTO: Jay Whitecombe

Opposite
TITLE: My Family
MATERIAL: Knitted objects
DATE: 2008
PHOTO: Rachel Smith

HelenAmyMurray works with fabric as a blank canvas for creating her luxurious and decorative low-relief designs.

After graduation her first exhibition of works was at the 100% Design Exhibition in 2003. Helen uses her name as her logo, and classes herself as a designer, maker and artist, which allows her to be diverse and conceptual whilst still having an eye for function. Once you come into contact with a piece by Murray you clearly see the perfection of her skills and labour.

Carefully cut, raised and stitched geometric forms grace the surface of the leather and textiles, showcasing her high-design and couture approach to surface manipulation. Her collections follow themes such as flowers and plants, birds and animals, and geometric shapes. She says her inspiration comes from growing up in the country as a child and living in the city as an adult. 'Nature and the natural world is the main inspiration behind my work, and this leads to more abstract patterns and surreal ideas.'

Every piece Murray creates is a unique design to fulfil the demands of each commission. However, each one follows a repeatable process and adheres to the same principles of application.

Her armchair, nursing chair and tub chair collections transform classic chair shapes into pieces of art, with her manipulated textiles adorning the sides and backs.

In 2003, Helen won the overall prize at the Oxo Peugeot Design Awards, and was part of the NESTA Creative Pioneer Programme. 'This significantly helped me towards setting up my first studio and making more work for exhibitions,' she says.

Helen has the drive for business and the ability to forge collaborations that will further her success. In 2009, she won the Homes and Gardens Classic Design Award for a collaborative project with The Rug Company in the creation of the Peony Rug, which is produced using New Zealand wool and uses pile cut to different heights to give depth and distinction to the pattern.

Helen works in her design studio with a small team of dedicated craftspeople to assist in the production of works, and she also sources local upholstery companies.

'I used to make all of my pieces alone, but as my work became recognised this became impossible. I now focus on design and I have a production manager, although everything is still finished by hand in my London studio.'

Helen is reinventing fabric and brings opulence, beauty and tactility to the surfaces she creates. Her advice for other designers who may wish to start up their own practice is, 'Good photography is really important for sending to press, potential clients and for a strong website. I started off doing it myself, but the quality wasn't anywhere near as strong as the professional images I now have taken. Keep on top of accounts and tax matters. Follow your instincts and stick to your principles. Don't be talked into doing things you don't want to do if your heart's not in it.

'Try to make time for your creative development as it becomes harder with the pressures and responsibilities of running a business.

'As your business develops so should your openness to taking on valuable work placements: students are eager to gain experience, it lightens the load, and you shouldn't be working 24 hours a day!'

Opposite
TITLE: 'Oriental' Wall–
mounted Artwork
MATERIAL: 100% wool felt
DATE: 2007
PHOTO: Marcos Bevilacqua

Top right
TITLE: Danish Tub Chair
'Peacock'
MATERIAL: Novasuede
DATE: 2007
PHOTO: Marcos Bevilacqua

Stella Corrall UK

TEXTILE DESIGNER: BREAKING THE MOULD

Textile designer Stella Corrall is perhaps better described as a fabric technologist. She is a designer and maker, but takes it one step further and actually creates the material from which her products are made.

Stella's work is created through laborious processes which have been perfected in her search for new materials, techniques and processes, whilst also being conscious of the needs of product design. Using mainly a self-manufactured flexible plastic, her work combines permanent surface decoration and temporary installations for interiors. She also develops her materials with function in mind and finds ways of incorporating her 'self-made' materials into products for the design- and eco-conscious consumer.

Stella explains the development of her interest in working with plastic, 'In my second year of study whilst at university I used a flexible plastic for a stool seat as part of a joint furniture project. I got hooked on experimenting with and dyeing this vinyl in the textile lab, and subsequently worked with it for the rest of my degree. Since then I have continued to develop techniques and processes by myself and then, more progressively, with the support of contacts in the plastics recycling industry.'

Stella's businesses started in 2000, when she began to further her research for finding suitable sources of discarded waste material, which in turn fuelled the production of her designs. 'My products use locally sourced redundant materials which would otherwise be headed for landfill. Materials in production are used extremely economically,

with minimal waste. Production is carried out locally, keeping down the impact of transportation on the environment.'

Sustainability often compromises design. It is rare to find a product made from recycled materials which has managed to conceal its origins. Stella has turned this challenge on its head in making a product collection which celebrates its reclaimed sources rather than trying to pretend otherwise. 'My inspiration comes naturally from a desire to produce sustainable, recycled products whilst capturing individuality yet not compromising my design ethic,' she says.

In 2007, the home and lifestyle retailer Habitat approached Stella to create a bespoke collection of recycled products consisting of placemats and coasters, and in 2009 new collections of lighting were launched into an ever-expanding marketplace for ethical product design.

Stella also produces artwork, which is used in

Left
TITLE: Archive Fabric Coaster
MATERIAL: Recycled flexible plastic and vintage fabric
DATE: 2009
PHOTO: Sara Porter

Right
TITLE: Free-standing Screen with bespoke plastic design commissioned by LIME for patient area
MATERIAL: Self-produced bespoke plastic
DATE: 2009
PHOTO: Stella Corrall

a number of different applications and environments, from wall hangings in private collections to bespoke installations in the offices of the BBC in London. There is an air of serenity that comes through the surface designs of her installations. It is therefore no surprise to see her client list includes healthcare trusts, where rooms are designed for recovery and relaxation.

Her advice for the next generation of designers is 'to challenge yourself to work more with recycled materials that can be made into aesthetic solutions so that the consumer can shed their belief that recycled means low quality.

'The new underpinning ethos for the 21st century designer has got to be an understanding of issues of sustainablility. The increase in volumes of waste diverted from landfill will provide new materials for designers to recycle into aesthetically satisfying and functional new products.

'Enjoy yourself, be determined and network with others.'

Below

TITLE: Lace Shade

MATERIAL: Reclaimed lace and plastic

DATE: 2009

PHOTO: Sara Porter

Teresa Green is the name of the printed textile company, but Teresa Cole is the maker behind the name. Teresa creates imagery of a life you wished you had.

Parisian cloches that cover fairy cakes or romantic scenes of line-drawn boats, chirping birds and their cages, and old cutlery. As an illustrator this designer creates snapshots of life adorned by freshly baked bread and old flour shakers. Teresa is perhaps an unsung illustrator, although a celebrated textile designer. Her ability to create marriages between textiles, illustration and typography invites the observer into a world that appeals to both traditional and contemporary audiences alike.

Teresa exhibited her first collection at the New Designers Exhibition in London in 2001 as part of One Year On, a satellite event hosted by the Crafts Council. This led to the setting-up of her studio in 2002. Her product collections cover all of the home elements: cooking, eating, sleeping and most recently children's clothes. Bedspreads and cushions, aprons and tea towels, bibs and baby-grows have all been carefully produced in the UK and hand-printed in her studio using traditional print techniques.

'I love the process because it is so instant, explains Teresa. The quality of the mark will change depending on pressure, retaining something of the maker. The variety with the medium can be as simple as potato printing and hand carving, but can achieve really exciting results. I also love the faded sense of time achieved with years of washing.'

Teresa has sourced some financial support for her business and design progression. This includes assistance from the Crafts Council in the form of a setting-up grant and from the Prince's Trust for start-up funding, as well as mid-career support through the Arts Council England and from Design Factory, the creative development agency based in the East Midlands.

Teresa's work sells to a diverse array of prestigious retailers, which is a compliment to her illustrative styles and an ability to cross-reference her audiences. Retailers include Designers Guild in London, John Derian Store in New York and HP Deco in Tokyo.

Inspiration is drawn from what she calls, 'the simplicity of the everyday'.

She further elaborates, 'I look at the traditional proportions of household objects, depicting an essence of them rather than a photographic interpretation. Each piece is screen-printed by

Right
TITLE: Waist Apron 'Plate Design'
MATERIAL: Irish linen
DATE: 2008
PHOTO: Alan Duncan

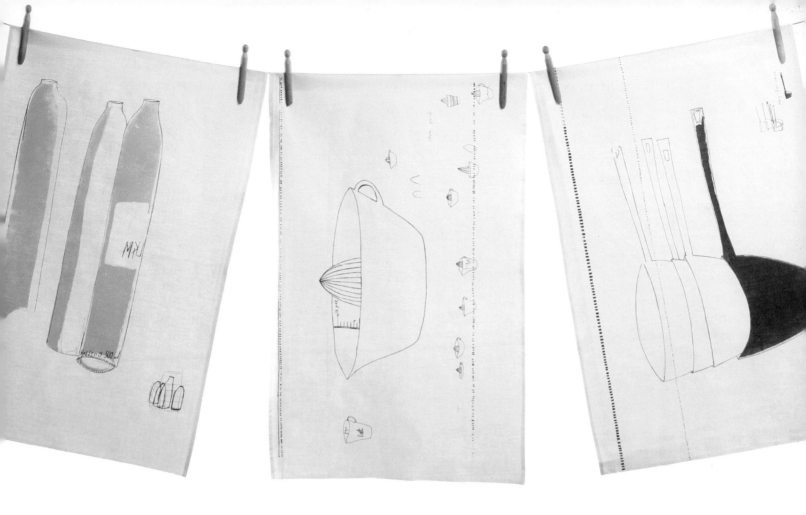

hand, enjoying the uniqueness and error that hand registration gives, whilst I am interested in the duality of a piece being both an artwork and a functional item.'

Her helpful tips for the next generation of textile designers are, 'Push yourself to go for it – there is no reason you cannot succeed if you really want it enough.

'Contact the Crafts Council or the Arts Council for support and advice. Ask other makers/designers – networking is the easiest way to find out things.

'Plan ahead, value your time, and price your work for what it's worth, not what you can afford to pay.'

Above
TITLE: Tea Towels; Milk Bottles, Lemon Squeezer and Pans
MATERIAL: Hand-printed cotton
DATE: 2006
PHOTO: Alan Duncan

Left
TITLE: Laundry Bag Bird Cage Design
MATERIAL: Linen
DATE: 2007
PHOTO: Alan Duncan

Metal and Jewellery

Our appetite for metal and jewellery has never been greater as designers and makers encapsulate the skill of working with metal and precious metals through contemporary design.

The designer is challenging our perception of this hard-to-manipulate material through organic forms, soft lines and tactile textures in the creation of objets d'art, objects to be worn and objects for the home.

Designer-maker studios are being developed in disused jewellery quarters across the UK, whilst the skill set of those most experienced in their craft is being preserved through schemes, guilds and organisations and through knowledge sharing up and down the country.

The result is a strong community of both makers and consumers who have an empathy for the craft behind the object, for each soldered join and piercing-sawed part of metal.

There are also the deconstructionists who are taking apart the craft behind metalwork and merging this with technology – water-jet cutting, laser and moulded-metal production – in the creation of new works which in themselves offer new price points and new audiences.

Metal designers have often played with human interaction within their work, but there is a new breed who are playing with emotion, wit, dialect and humour, often blurring fine-art principles with craft outcomes. For some designers this enables a declassification of the preciousness of metal, whilst others are producing work traditionally with new accents celebrating contemporary design, fighting back on behalf of people who have become accustomed to cheap products within a disposable society.

The metalworker fossilises current trends and offers us something to feel special about which can be passed down for generations.

Opposite
TITLE: Gold Earstuds
ARTIST: Jane Adam
MATERIAL: 22 Carat Gold
and 128 carat green gold
with rough diamonds.
DATE: 2008
PHOTO: Joel Degen

Ane Christensen was born in Copenhagen and is now based in London, where she set up her business and studio after graduating in 1999.

Ane produces silver tableware as well as larger-scale sculptural vessels. She makes her batch-produced items by herself without outside manufacturing help, which enables her to tailor them to a scale that suits each individual client.

'I have been drawn to precious metals and jewellery since I was a child,' Ane says. 'As a teenager, I found a piece of copper on a building site, tried to make my own jewellery and started dreaming of becoming a goldsmith.'

Like many others, Ane received financial help from both the Crafts Council and the National Association of Goldsmiths, which allowed her to follow her own path when she graduated. She also became associated with design groups like Design Nation and the Danish Silversmiths Association, which helped her to approach other designers within both her own field and others.

In 2005, Ane was shortlisted for the Jerwood Applied Arts Prize at the Crafts Council in London, and went on to win the Best New Merchandise award presented by the Goldsmiths' Company in the City of London.

Ane challenges our assumptions about precious metals and creates objects of desire which lend themselves to being sculptures that also happen to be functional pieces – bowls, candlesticks and the like. 'Each piece takes advantage of the tension and memory of the metal. The result is more concerned with the qualities of sculpture and surprise than with pure functionality.'

Her ability to blur the boundaries of art and craft has led to the creation of works which leave the viewer looking at not only the finished piece of work but also realising the amount of time and attention to detail Ane has dedicated to each object. She explains her working process: 'Each design begins in paper, and I aim to capture the crisp and light quality of the paper when translating into metal. The pieces add both drama and everyday functionality to the dining table.'

Inspired by paper and strands of ribbon which

create beauty and movement, Ane's work is both a centrepiece and a conversation piece. Although created as functional objects, her series of bowls and other vessels are nothing short of works of art.

Ane's advice for other designers who may wish to start up their own practice is, 'Manage your cash flow very carefully.

'Do not supply too many galleries too quickly. It is better to have larger groups of work in fewer places.

'Try to have a few projects on the go at all times – when one "gets stuck", carry on with something else.

'In my experience, if nothing sells, panicking and making cheaper pieces does not work. A better, though scarier, solution is to make bolder, more confident, bespoke pieces instead.'

Finally, Ane adds, 'I would never recommend having a part-time job whilst setting up your own business. It puts huge strain on your time and making money from your own work suddenly doesn't seem so urgent. It is always better to be poor and focused!'

Opposite
TITLE: Fragments No.1
MATERIAL: Patinated copper
DATE: 2005
PHOTO: Courtesy of the artist

Above right
TITLE: Dented Bowl
MATERIAL: Patinated copper
DATE: 2005
PHOTO: Courtesy of the artist

Right
TITLE: Crumbling
MATERIAL: Sterling silver
DATE: 2006
PHOTO: Frank Thurston and Sussie Ahlburg

It was when Jane started to experiment with non-precious metals that her work became known to a wider contemporary audience, and her anodised aluminium is now immediately recognisable.

Jane Adam is perhaps best described as an alchemist of the studio-jewellery world. Her work is an eclectic mix of form and pattern with a sophistication which makes you want to talk about, hold, touch and wear her objects of adornment. Working with chemical reactions and how metals respond to different surface applications, Jane has over years of experimentation created some of the most recognisable items of jewellery to emerge from the contemporary British jewellery scene. She says,

'I work with materials to find out what they will do, and push them to their limits to exploit their inherent qualities: the way a metal crazes or tears under stress, or how certain colours blend together as inks on a metal surface or on the screen of the computer.'

Jane's background has always been synonymous with craft and design. She gained an early insight into design from her parents, who were both trained in art. Her father was a graphic designer and illustrator and the family home reflected her parents' passion for craft and design, with furniture from Heal's and cutlery by Gense (the Swedish design house established in 1856, acknowledged masters of metal-cutlery design and form). This inherited knowledge of design is something she carries with her to this day, together with her passion for craft and for wanting to make something with her own hands.

Between 1972 and 1977 she worked as the retail manager for Heal's and then Liberty, and later, in 1985, gained an MA in Metalwork and Jewellery from the Royal College of Art. The same year she was granted the Crafts Council Setting Up Grant to start her own business. But as Jane recalls, college education was a time of learning about herself as much as the practices of art and design: 'When I started on my foundation course I knew I wanted to design and make, but wasn't sure what.'

It was when she started to experiment with non-precious metals that her work became known to a wider contemporary audience. Her experiments with surface design and the anodisation and coloration of aluminium, together with how metals could be stressed, distorted and manipulated, gave rise to much new work.

'For nearly 30 years, I have involved myself in innovation and experimentation with anodised

Below left

TITLE: Pod Brooches
MATERIAL: Fine silver, sterling silver and 18 carat gold. Oxidisation with undyed, cultured freshwater pearls
DATE: 2006
PHOTO: Joel Degen

Below

TITLE: 'Urban' Spiral Bangles
MATERIAL: Dyed anodised aluminium
DATE: 2009
PHOTO: Joel Degen

aluminium, to create a repertoire of new processes of dyeing, mark-making, crazing and texturing and forming. Thus, from a dull industrial material, I create something new and unexpected, jewellery with its own kind of beauty and preciousness.'

Jane works with anodised aluminium sheet, silver, copper and gold, and ensures that she makes at least some of each piece herself. 'My gesture is an important part of the piece,' she explains.

Jane knows her audience well, having grown with them through the 30 years she has been practising as a jeweller, yet she is successfully attracting new generations towards her work as she develops new processes and draws inspiration from the present.

Jane sells her work to over 50 outlets in the UK, USA and Japan, including Contemporary Applied Arts in London, the Scottish Gallery in Edinburgh and Velvet da Vinci in San Francisco.

When asked for advice for new designers her reply was, 'The circumstances are so different now from when I started – there is much more support available, and many more good outlets, but financially it is much tougher to get started.

'When you do start, the one resource you have is time. You just have to keep going, keep trying, observe what happens to your work when it reaches the market, listen to what people (buyers, the public, etc.) are saying and how they react to what you are offering them. Learn from it, understand what they are saying and why, let it become part of your design brief, if you like, but don't be dominated by it. In the end, you must let your voice be heard, particularly if it is saying something worth listening to.'

Above

TITLE: Leaf Necklace
MATERIAL: Dyed anodised aluminium, stainless steel and labradorites
DATE: 2006
PHOTO: Joel Degen

'Most of my pieces are one-offs,' says Sidsel, 'and usually the process develops from one piece to the next, so that each piece raises questions and challenges which I then try to explore in the next.'

Manipulating delicate wafer-thin wraps of silver elegantly falling over forms and vessels has become a hallmark for Sidsel Dorph-Jensen, as has her perfectionism, her skill and her beautiful handling of precious metals and the craft of the silversmith. Sidsel graduated from the Royal College of Art in 2003, where she studied silversmithing, but in 2002, whilst still studying on the course, she was presented with The Worshipful Company of Goldsmiths Young Designer – Silversmith Award. She subsequently set up her studio and workshop in North London, though today this is based in Denmark, where she also has a showroom.

Sidsel makes all of the pieces herself and uses precious metals to explore her aesthetics of tactility, weightlessness, movement and decorative form. She explains that 'The malleability of silver fascinates me, the way you can hammer a rod into a spoon, or raise a flat sheet into a vase or bowl.'

In the piece titled *Cherry Bowl* Sidsel demonstrates her delicate yet bold approach to working with metal.'The thin silver sheets have to do with strength and perception. I really like the way the combination of the thin sheets makes the objects look light or weightless (even if they are not), but at the same time repeating the sheets makes it a really strong construction. The concept of construction in any object, be it an organism, material or vegetation, is of great inspiration to me. I find the way the structure of different units can create form, volume and space very interesting and I enjoy exploring silver and its properties, its malleability in complex constructions and different surface textures.'

Sidsel sells her work mainly to galleries but works with clients on bespoke collections and commissions. In 2006, it was a commission from New College, Oxford which allowed her to explore further the qualities of precious materials, in this case silver and gold.

Her work entitled Fingerbowl combined the hard properties of metal with thin ribbon-like structures that flow through, and also subdivide, the bowl's interior. The brief stipulated that any decoration should be on the inside of the bowl. Sidsel explains, 'The bowl is used for water to wet your fingers in after having eaten lobster. The water flows freely through the different compartments in the bowl, and makes very interesting reflections in the gilded surface.'

In 2008, she created *Bowl No 5*. The bowl was made by manipulating the silver and creating a series of five bowls, all slightly smaller in size, which fit perfectly inside one another. The effect is that the rims of the bowls begin to resemble the edges of ripped paper, distorted yet under perfect control.

'Most of my pieces are one-offs,' she says, 'and usually process develops from one piece to the next, so that one piece raises questions and challenges which I then try to explore in the next piece.'

Sidsel's advice for the next generation of designers is, 'Research your market thoroughly before starting so you know your colleagues and competitors well, and know where to place yourself.

'The first couple of years is about testing you and the market – do as many shows, exhibitions, retail outlets, etc. as possible, then you know which ones to focus on and it's a good way to launch.

'Know your limitations and pay for services you're not good at (such as accounting, graphics, photography, etc.). Then you can focus on what you do best.'

SIDSEL DORPH-JENSEN

103

Calm and collected aesthetics combined with precious materials, lead to the creation of artefacts you want to treasure.

Based in London, Angela Cork's work is sculptural yet functional. Her work aspires towards perfection in execution and purveys purity and tranquillity through form and function. Angela creates objects that adorn interiors and spaces.

Angela graduated from the Royal College of Art in 2002, where she studied her MA in Silversmithing, and in 2004 was awarded the Crafts Council Development Award, which helped build the foundations of her practice and business.

Whilst Angela plays with negative space and the harsh outlines of metal to create what appear to be three-dimensional line drawings, her silverware has a tactile feeling.

'I strive to make objects that have a presence, and although I design with function in mind, it is also important for me to see my objects as sculpture,' explains Angela.

When you look at Angela's work you are immediately drawn towards the level of craft and skill she employs in the creation of her pieces. Transforming the harsh surface of the metal into a soft finish is important to her in the final piece, as is the juxtaposition of balance and movement.

'I find the substance and malleability of metal satisfying to work with. I like its hardness, permanence and how it starts as a rough material that can be worked and finished to become something finely executed. The variety of techniques that can be used to shape and form fascinates me, as do the effects you can produce.'

The balance of space and form plays an important role in Angela's metal work. For the collection entitled Frame Vase Angela appears to offer a miniature environment which houses a single flower stem, suggesting the illusion that the vase is part of a bigger picture, placed on a windowsill perhaps or upon a shelf. With the Outline Balloon Vase, the sterling silver form has been designed to gently rock on a surface whilst keeping the flower stem in position, held to accompany the vase as it moves from side to side.

Her collections have been exhibited widely in the UK including the Goldsmiths Fair in London and through Collect, the international art fair for contemporary objects, hosted by the Crafts

Right

TITLE: Waterline Vase
MATERIAL: Sterling Silver, part oxidised
DATE: 2008
PHOTO: Sussie Ahlburg

Above

TITLE: Frame Vases

MATERIAL: Sterling silver, one oxidised

DATE: 2008

PHOTO: Sussie Ahlburg

Council, which runs each year in London.

Her pieces of advice for the next generation of designers are, 'Apply for funding and initially buy only what you need.'

Press plays an important role in the life of any designer: 'Make sure you have good images of your work.'

'Have a five-year plan and make considered ranges of work — well-executed bodies of work sell better.' And finally, 'Identify your market.' Who do you want to sell to and how do you envisage selling it?

Above

TITLE: Outline Balloon Vase

MATERIAL: Sterling silver– part-oxidised

DATE: 2004

PHOTO: Frank Thurston

Left

TITLE: Slim Vases

MATERIAL: Sterling silver, one oxidised

DATE: 2004

PHOTO: Courtesy of artist

In Rebecca's world, we find books with people who appear to be walking to work, oblivious to the fact that they are simply being used as the top of a bookmark.

Rebecca Joselyn creates everyday objects such as plates, bookmarks or bowls, bringing them to life by adding reference points which turn them into miniature worlds of conversation and interaction with the people who use them.

Rebecca graduated from university in 2006, but in her final year was awarded a Precious Metal Bursary through the Goldsmiths' Company. She was later offered a studio space to continue her work in Sheffield, where she is now based.

The way in which people relate to objects plays a key role in Rebecca's work. In 2006, she began to embark on a journey using precious metals to transform discarded, apparently worthless items of rubbish into timeless works of art which successfully combine function and sculpture. This culminated in a series entitled Packaging. For instance, a crumpled crisp packet was reproduced using silver sheet. The silver sheets were worked with a mallet to convey the creases and folds of the original crisp packet. The piece is entitled Crisp Bowl, denoting a new function that is only removed from its original use by virtue of the value of the new material and the skilled craftsmanship needed to shape it.

Drinking straws, ice-cream containers and even a string bag which once contained fruit have been frozen in time using precious metals. Rebecca explains that 'our lifestyles of convenience and throwaway items have become a major source of inspiration for me'.

Inevitably, the design of these pieces also evokes the spectre of commercialism, as these are all objects with which we associate and live our lives, and then dump in landfill sites. Rebecca's transformation of these mundane items into objects of beauty is both an ironic commentary on our trashy society and a reminder that beauty can be found in even the most unlikely places.

One of her most engaging collections is the series she calls People, in which tiny human figures adorn otherwise conventional everyday objects (see also p.13). There is something romantic about turning an inanimate object such as a plate into a miniature world – a pavement or plaza – where people interact, making you ask questions such as what these two characters could be talking about, and are they aware they are living their lives on a plate? (See p.127.)

In this miniature world we also find books with people who appear to be walking to work, oblivious to the fact that they are simply being used as the top of a bookmark, or a lady sitting cross-legged on a stool that is actually the top of a cocktail stick. These are witty and poignant pieces that evoke childhood memories and times when people would stop and talk to one another in the street.

Rebecca's advice for other designers wishing to start their own practice is, 'Work hard and don't give up easily – it takes a few years before things really start to happen.'

Opposite above
TITLE: Fruit Bag
MATERIAL: Silver
DATE: 2007
PHOTO: Paula Kirby

Right
TITLE: Screwball
MATERIAL: Silver
DATE: 2008
PHOTO: Paula Kirby

Far right
TITLE: People Bookmark
MATERIAL: Silver
DATE: 2008
PHOTO: Jerry Lampson

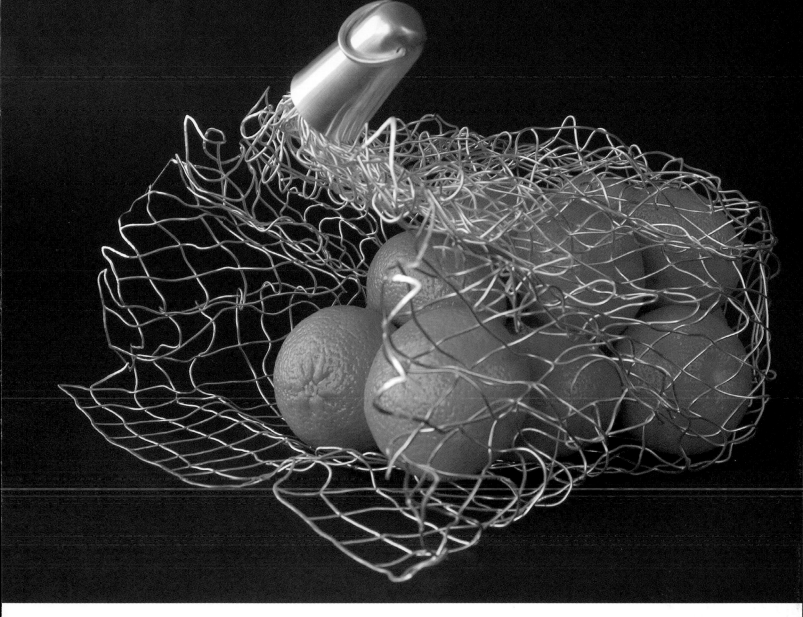

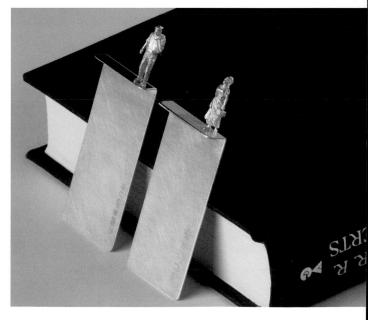

REBECCA JOSELYN

Surface design
AND DECORATION

In the last decade we have seen a transition from white-walled living spaces to the embracing of wallpapers, surface design and pattern into our lives.

The 2000s saw consumer trends bringing pattern back into the home on a scale last witnessed with the Eames Era of the 1950s. Flock wallpaper even made its return with wallpaper houses such as London-based Cole and Son becoming the visionaries for setting trends for both lifestyles and interiors.

There is one drastic difference in the new style however, when compared to the ideals which predecessors in pattern brought to the table — and that is scale. Today's players in pattern are using scale like never before. Repeat print is being replaced with bold statements and bold imagery. Actual-size telephone boxes and postboxes are being utilised in wallpapers, whilst tactility and interaction between person and product is fuelling the designer's appetite for pushing boundaries, techniques and processes.

The designers are offering a snapshot of the outdoors indoors, with photographic panels of nature, landscapes and life beyond the four walls which once housed tablemats with plain colours for beige interiors. Today photography, digital imagery and traditional screen-printing are all being fused together whilst the designer concentrates on engaging the spectator through textures and hand-applied details.

Surface pattern and decoration is enjoying a strong revival which will ensure that it is here to stay. Designers are drawing inspiration from new subject matters and materials, and engaging new approaches in creating pattern from walls to floors and from paper to product.

Opposite

TITLE: Blink!

ARTIST: Ilias Fotopoulos

MATERIAL: Hand printed and flocked non-woven base: red flock on white, black flock on white

DATE: 2008

PHOTO: Michael Kai

Wallpaper designer Deborah Bowness has an eye for photography, and for how she can turn her photographic images into startling collections of wallpapers.

Deborah's wallpapers are now among the most sought-after interior-design fashion statements of the early 21st century. Over the past few years, since being awarded a Crafts Council grant to set up her studio, she has plundered our collective memories of all kinds of interior spaces to create disconcerting environments that make us do a double take as we enter them. What appear to be filing cabinets or bookshelves or cupboards with clothes hanging out of them turn out to be the witty illusions of this highly original artist.

Below

TITLE: Standard Lamps Wallpaper

MATERIAL: Digital and silkscreen on wallpaper

DATE: 2004

PHOTO: Deb Bowness

'I started working with wallpaper as a way of making my art useful,' explains Deborah. 'Wallpaper provides a functional surface to put an image onto. Repeating in pattern is not important to me. Creating an illusion is where my interest lies. The first piece I produced utilises *trompe l'oeil* frocks and real hooks to further the 2D into a 3D illusion. Using wallpaper allows presence within a space. By manipulating and placing familiar imagery on the paper I create an unfamiliar presence. The images I use are sourced from a collection of my own photography.'

Deborah's intention to capture future trends through the lens of a camera and transform these into 'useful pieces of art' has propelled her towards new audiences and environments where wallpaper would have usually been seen as too traditional or uninspiring.

Enlivened by what she describes as 'other

Above

TITLE: Illusions of Grandeur

MATERIAL: Digital and silkscreen printing on wallpaper

DATE: 2003

PHOTO: Deb Bowness

people's possessions and the objects we surround ourselves with', these collections of wallpaper evoke a vague sense of nostalgia for something we have allowed to escape our minds.

'My ideas come sporadically, generally when I am least expecting them. I have been finding and collecting objects for many years. Charity and second-hand shops are rich in inspiration,' explains Deborah.

Deborah's work is a blend of machine- and man-made art. She was among the first designers to experiment with digital processes of manufacturing, and her wallpaper is produced by combining digital images with silkscreen printing. She then adds hand-painted details to create unique, scratchy finishes. Her clever use of scale, repeat pattern and segregation of the design – for example, having one printed drop of wallpaper against three or four plain drops – can't fail to create unique spaces.

Her client list is a testimony to her talent. Commissions Deborah has worked on adorn our high-street stores and the coolest of retailers. From fashion houses such as Paul Smith and Lacroix to the hip cafes of Norway, Deborah uses walls as though they were blank canvases made ready for her snapshots of everyday life.

Her advice for the next generation of designers is, 'Maintain a high quality and keep the essence of your concept in everything you do.

'Never handle the same piece of paper twice, for instance, open a letter and deal with it straight away.

'Keep your overheads to a minimum, and keep your cash flow flowing.

'And remember that every business is different. If it's your own you can run things to suit yourself although there are a few issues (mainly accounting) that are standard.'

Above

TITLE: Plan, Tool and Filing Draws Wallpaper

MATERIAL: Digital and silkscreen printing on wallpaper

DATE: 2004

PHOTO: Deb Bowness

Ilias Fotopoulos is an experimental designer and artist working with surface pattern and design. In 2008 he won the acclaimed Bombay Sapphire Design Discovery Award for his wall-covering collections.

Ilias creates his fabrics by abstracting beauty from textures which portray decay and human interaction. He initially studied law but in his designs he rebels against order by drawing inspiration from nature's chaos. Ilias started his studio in 2003 after realising that textiles were not being explored through surface manipulation. Textiles offered him a blank canvas for experimenting with mark-making, creating textures that encapsulate the effects time wreaks in nature and in our built environments.

Being provoked by textures fuels this designer's work, which includes wallpapers, textiles and products such as cushions and notebooks. 'My professional interest in textiles started as a student. I was unable to find the fabrics I could see in my imagination. Driven by need, I conducted experiments applying lacquers, heat and acids in controlled and uncontrolled ways. I would dye, shred and reconfigure the results, creating completely new textures.'

Ilias uses mark-making ideas often deemed as 'errors' to inspire his work. 'Mistakes and matters that we may normally reject or seek to rectify' are recorded through surface pattern and repeat

Left

TITLE: Acid Etch Wallpaper

MATERIAL: Hand printed metallic laminated non- woven base

DATE: 2008

PHOTO: Michael Kai

design, which he uses to create products for personal use, homes and interiors.

From the tiny circles left behind by hole-punchers to the marks braille makes when offering the written word to the blind, Ilias takes pleasure in using discarded information to fuel his ideas.

'My mother would work for days creating garments with intricate details painstakingly by hand. Use of her hands in this way was an incredible skill to me, and I would watch patiently, asking questions and waiting for the end result, which was made without a pattern and always beautiful.

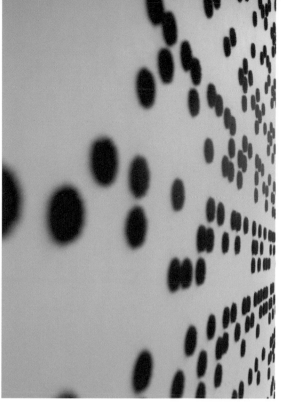

Left

TITLE: Listen and Record, wallpaper in braille

MATERIAL: Hand-printed and flocked, non-woven base, red flock on white

DATE: 2008

PHOTO: Ilias Fotopoulos

Below

TITLE: Growing/Falling, wallpaper (shown hung as Falling)

MATERIAL: Hand-printed non-woven wallpaper, red flock on white

DATE: 2009

PHOTO: Jessica Mattino

I am certain that this is why creating with my hands is a natural part of me. Some things are handed down.'

Ilias's first exhibition was in 2007 at the 100% Design Tokyo exhibition, and in 2008 he showcased his work at the same organisation's London exhibition.

Although based in Sydney, Australia, Ilias manages a manufacturing process with skilled craft makers thousands of miles away from his own studio and workshop.

'I now pass on my ideas and research to skilled craftspeople to manufacture in England and Japan. All the work is hand-printed, and this was an important aspect to me. Machine printing gave the advantage of production that was faster and about one fifth of my current production costs, but keeping skilled artisans working is an important aspect of sustainability that is often overlooked.'

Ilias's advice to the next generation of designers is, 'Be original from the initial conception of an idea through to the final piece.

'I also teach and find it disturbing that most students I see do their visual research on a computer and from magazines. Computers are a great tool but they are just a tool. They cannot take the place of the hand and mind connection. You are, no matter what program you use, limited to the predefined actions of the program.'

Finally Ilias adds, 'I strongly encourage designers to work more as artists, exploring feelings through a variety of media and most importantly getting their hands dirty.'

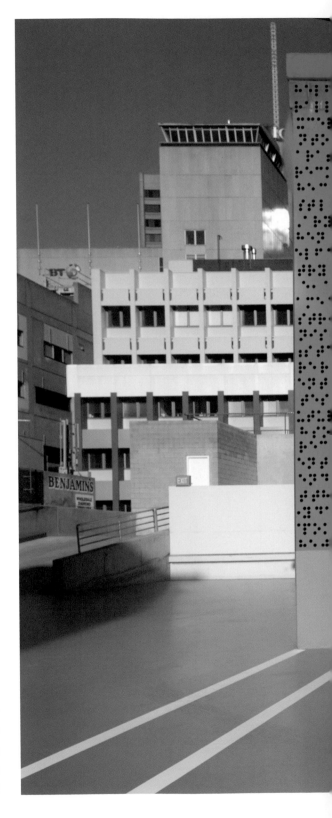

Right

TITLE: Listen and Record, wallpaper in braille
MATERIAL: Hand-printed non-woven base, black 3D medium
DATE: 2009
PHOTO: Michael Kai

Tracy Kendall has an experimental approach towards surface decoration, a result of her training, through which she became part fine artist and part printmaker.

Tracy's approach towards surface decoration involves using large-scale photographic imagery of objects such as cutlery, feathers and flowers to create walls of distinction and beauty. Tracy's initial art training was as a fine-art printmaker. The fine art side of Kendall drives the desire for creating one-off pieces but the printmaker side of her training wants to be able to experiment with repeat pattern and duplicating images to create patterns.

'I also like the technical challenges involved in making reproducible work, challenging the component parts of the design, the structure, and the build. I was also taught on my MA by an embroidery tutor who introduced me to bringing in new elements to wall coverings.'

She launched her wallpaper at the 100% Design exhibition in 1997. She works from her studio in London creating in-house collections and also bespoke series for clients in the UK and else-

where, selling to well-respected boutiques such as The Collection in Paris, Ted Boerner in America and South Pacific Fabrics in Australia.

When asked where inspiration is drawn from, she replies, 'anywhere and everywhere', which perhaps explains why the range of imagery and textures across her collections is so diverse, from the aforementioned old knives and forks to intricate buttons which have been hand-applied to the surface of the wallpaper. This random accumulation of source objects is redolent of the scavenging approach of the American artist Joseph Cornell.

Tracy is not afraid of experimentation, and challenges the prescribed function of objects by coating the wallpaper surfaces with tiny circular pieces of plastic and even jigsaw pieces. Her Sequin collection, for example, which was inspired by 1920s flapper dresses, found her applying individual sequins to objects such as shelves and Robin Day chairs.

'All of the designs are refined to their simplest form so that you only see the main driving idea and not the support or the constraints of the material or process,' explains Kendall.

Tracy believes that wallpapers should be challenging and should engage with the environment and the users of that environment. 'I use a wide range of techniques for my work – hand and digital printing as well as hand and digital stitching – so that I am not tied to one method of production. The design can be carried out in its best production method rather than the only production method, allowing the design to show its full qualities.'

Left

TITLE: Sequins

MATERIAL: Non-woven hand-printed wallpaper with plastic sequins attached

DATE: 2000

PHOTO: Rachel Smith

Below
TITLE: In The Whiteroom   DATE: 2001
MATERIAL: Wallpaper stitched   PHOTO: Courtesy of the artist
with polyester thread

In 2002, Tracy embarked on a new method of creating wall surfaces. Her stand at 100% Design stood out on account of her clean and tactile approach to applying a pattern to the walls, which played with the senses and re-imagined the inter-action between a wall and the environment it helps to shape. The series was called Stripe, and used paper and stitch to create three-dimensional wall-paper which moved as air circulated around the folds and cuts in the paper.

Her series Fringe, created in 2007, comprised hand-stitched wallpaper using embroidery fringes that was reminiscent of theatrical curtains and baroque decoration.

It was Tracy's embroidery tutor who also showed her how to time herself when creating work. She was able to formulate how she could get a price on her labour and make the work cost-effective. 'Your time is your most valuable commodity'.

The secret of her success is the same as the advice she offers to new designers:

'Have passion for everything that you do – it shows in the work at all times. Have commitment. Put all your energy into it.

'Be flexible – if the day, the week, the piece doesn't always work out how you plan, that may sometimes be a good thing.

'And finally, take risks – they could be the making of you and your work.'

Right
TITLE: Button Chair   DATE: 2004
MATERIAL: Polypropylene   PHOTO: Courtesy of the
chair with buttons attached artist

Ella Doran's work is both contemporary and timeless, colourful and playful.

Ella's work can be found in many retail outlets from the local high street to the metropolitan design boutique as well as in her own shop in Cheshire Street, London.

After graduating from university with a degree in textiles, Ella travelled to Africa on a six-month work placement and took with her a camera to record her journey. 'I then started to realise that the images I was taking were designs in their own right'.

So Ella used a picture she had taken to create a collection of works called Pebbles, which consisted of a range of table mats, a malamine tray and earthenware products, with the image gracefully adorning the flat surfaces, bringing them to life. It was this collection which brought her recognition and established her business.

Like many designer-makers, Ella then showcased her work at the New Designers Exhibition in London, from which she obtained her first commission.

She became self-employed immediately after finishing her university course and in 1996 successfully applied for a loan from the Prince's Trust. This funding helped support the creation of further collections using 2D imagery taken on her travels on functional ware such as coasters and placemats.

Ella is a success story on many levels. Her work is recognised as among the most influential in surface design to have emerged over the last decade, whilst her level-headed passion for design seems immune to the accolades she receives from within the design world. Nevertheless, she is modest

Below

TITLE: Sunlight Through Leaves, G–Wiz Car
MATERIAL: Riva electric car
DATE: 2008
PHOTO: Courtesy of the artist

Opposite

TITLE: Award–winning shoe design (for John lewis Partnerships)
MATERIAL: Stationery, wrapping paper, boxes, note books and soft furnishings
DATE: 2006
PHOTO: Courtesy of the artist

Above
TITLE: Artists tools cut-out design
MATERIAL: Plastic tray
DATE: 2005
PHOTO: Courtesy of the artist

Opposite
TITLE: Georgia Blind
MATERIAL: Digitally printed polycotton
DATE: 2004
PHOTO: Courtesy of the artist

small to produce them for me.'

Much like her surface patterns, Ella's success also tells the story of a journey. Over the past 14 years she has evidently created not only a portfolio of imagery but also a close-knit community of manufacturing partners, from Cornwall in Southwest England, where her coasters are made, to Italy and Turkey, where she has discovered some of her materials.

This sense of community extends to being a member of Design Nation, which has assisted Ella in forming new links with industry names such as John Lewis. This door, as she recalls, was initially opened by the late and great Peta Levi of Design Nation, to whom this book is dedicated. Ella says that design-group initiatives such as Eureka and Hidden Art Select make the initial 'meet and greet' with businesses a lot easier.

Ella Doran is a great British design icon. Her inspiration stems from journeys, but perhaps most importantly from achieving her ultimate end goal, 'to make people smile'. She goes on, 'I am inspired by the everyday, my children, my memories and most of all what I capture with my camera. The best designs happen when I least expect them to'.

Her top tips for helping the next generation of designers are, 'to have an abundance of passion for what you do, as well as sufficient money and business support to guide you in your initial years of getting started.

'Launch your product when you are ready – not before or in a rush. It took me three years before I felt ready to properly set up my business after leaving college.

'Find the best trade show for your type of product as that is the best way to obtain contacts and make your statement. A trade show is your chance to stand out from the crowd.

'And finally, network everywhere you go.'

about what she has achieved. 'When I started I approached the challenge with gusto and no fear whatsoever. I look back and see that ignorance was bliss – now I apply more logic and it can sometimes be harder!'

Today Ella's award-winning portfolio of products crosses many disciplines, from ceramics to wallpaper, to bags, cushions and children's wear. 'I created the images and still do take all of the photographs. I started hand-making all the cushions and packaging for the coasters myself, but, with all of these products, as demand has grown I have sourced manufacturers both large and

The work of wallpaper artist Lizzie Allen is reminiscent of everything you wished you were old enough to remember if you are too young to have lived in the 1950s.

Outline drawings are splashed with primary colours. Blue skies and fluffy clouds are drawn and then printed with slight misalignment to capture what could be described as the illustrative movement made famous through children's storybooks and cartoons of the 1950s. This misalignment is also a consequence of the traditional hand-screenprint technique, where every print is unique. Welcome to the wonderful world of Lizzie Allen.

'As a kid I loved creating stories and characters, which has always stayed with me. The nostalgia of the 1950s always gets me – illustrators such as Mary Blair and Ludwig Bemelmans are fabulous. There's something about the feel of the fifties that I'm drawn to – the colours, the shapes,' explains Lizzie.

Before these wallpapers grace the interiors and boutiques of the design-conscious, each roll is hand-screenprinted either by Lizzie or using local traditional manufacturing processes in her home city of London. 'I've been brought up to appreciate our heritage and past and to engage in our future,' she says. 'It's important for me to combine the old and new. There are strong ties in my family with restoration, vintage and antiques, which is probably why you could find me haggling in a flea market for a good deal on a piece of fabric or something. I've also been fortunate to have travelled and lived in other parts of the world, such as New York and Dubai, which has been a real eye opener into other cultures and traditions, and has also made me really appreciate and love my own home, London.'

The 1950s however are not the only influence behind Lizzie's work. 'It's the everyday life, the places and people I see and visit, and routines, that intrigue me the most. I then describe what I see through drawing and printing.'

To be inspired by the past and design for the present is a common theme for the designer-maker. What is different with Lizzie's work, however, is that it retains a quality which could have been lifted out of a past generation, and for this reason the aesthetics which have been perfectly captured make the work fresh and contemporary for a new generation.

Lizzie launched her work at 100% Design in 2006, and followed this with an appearance at the Craft Council's Origin show. This was after having been awarded a place on the Crafts Council's Next Move Scheme in 2005.

Her glimpsed images of everyday life in a bygone age are meticulously realised in a way that is instantly evocative of the prim postwar period but without being pastiche. Commuters reading the *Daily Telegraph* or *London Gazette*, the Changing of the Guard and picture-postcard depictions of St Paul's Cathedral have all been frozen in time through her unique approach to surface pattern and design.

Lizzie Allen's helpful hints for new designers are, 'Be positive, be proactive and be persistent.

'Take every opportunity and every bit of advice that comes along.

'And finally, know your market and gain as much business knowledge as you can.'

Far left
TITLE: Red Buses and
Black Cabs
MATERIAL: Hand–
screenprinted wallpaper
DATE: 2008
PHOTO: Courtesy of the
artist

Left
TITLE: Telephone Box (Gold)
MATERIAL: Super–wide
hand–screenprinted
wallpaper
DATE: 2007
PHOTO: Courtesy of the
artist

Below, far right
TITLE: Telephone Box
MATERIAL: Super–wide
hand–screenprinted
wallpaper
DATE: 2007
PHOTO: Courtesy of the
artist

Below right
TITLE: Changing the
guards at Buckingham
Palace
MATERIAL: Hand–
sreenprinted wallpaper
DATE: 2006
PHOTO: Courtesy of the
artist

Opposite page
TITLE: Lizzie Allen's studio
PHOTO: John Carey

LIZZIE ALLEN

Behind the scenes

Behind the Scenes is an 'access all areas' invitation to advice and opinions from industry leaders within the craft, design and product arena. Carefully selected professionals from the creative community open their doors to answer questions which aim to offer the hand of support to the next generation of designers and makers.

Behind the Scenes interviews the press, the exhibition curator and the retailer whilst celebrating achievements in design, and finds out how they got to where they are in the design community, but most importantly asks how others can follow in their footsteps. Behind the Scenes offers an insight into the world of design, craft and product, which often hides behind glossy magazine covers and journalists' reviews.

Support for emerging talent is key to the fruition of the craft, design and product sector. Without sufficient support systems in place our emerging talents, who should be dictating the futures of craft, will be subject to turmoil, as will our industrial heritage.

For design lovers, design makers and design movers, this chapter is dedicated to people who want to make a difference, solve problems and push boundaries.

In the words of the late and great Peta Levi MBE, founder of Design Nation and the Design Trust, and to whom this entire book is dedicated. 'Introduce yourself to at least ten people that you have not met before'.

Opposite

TITLE: In the workspace at Design Glut

PHOTO: Courtesy of Design Glut

Rachel Moses

Rachel Moses of Design Nation acts as a point of contact for designers using its support system. It aims to promote British design and encourage young designers to get started.

Design-Nation is a not-for-profit organisation sited at Metropolitan Works, part of the London Metropolitan University. The aim of the organisation is to promote the excellence of British design whilst providing business advice to students and young designers and offering support to mid-career and established designers.

Design-Nation was set up by Peta Levi MBE in 1999 and is now championed by Rachel Moses, who continues to develop the organisation as its membership of designers and makers grows.

There is a selected membership of over 180 designers who are part of Design-Nation and tap into their support system, showcasing their work through the website and accompanying catalogue.

Membership is offered to five 3D disciplines: ceramics & glass; furniture; interior/exterior design & products; silver, gold, metalwork & jewellery; and textiles & fashion accessories. This portfolio is promoted to industry, specifiers, retailers, consumers and collectors.

Networking is essential for designers, and Design-Nation's Eureka networking project is instrumental in cultivating links with industry for its members.

In Rachel's own words, 'Design Nation initiated the Eureka Project to encourage retailers and manufacturers to commission products from members of the organisation. Two themes run through the project, firstly that design adds value to everyday objects, and secondly that there is an outstanding pool of creative talent based in Britain.' Designers such as Ella Doran, Ane Christensen, Margo Selby and I have all worked with retailers and manufacturers through the scheme.

Design Nation also offers 'Meet Design-Nation' networking events, which act as speed-dating for retailers, designers and manufacturers. As Rachel explains, 'Designers have benefited in a variety of

ways from attending the days, getting market intelligence or feedback on existing designs, on quality or cost, learning about another supplier that could assist in taking a design into production, gaining knowledge about production alternatives or new materials and meeting other designers with whom to collaborate on future projects'.

An example of a successful collaboration that resulted from a 'Meet design-Nation' event involved The Royal Festival Hall London which was made famous by both its architecture and for being home of the Festival of Britain which took place after the Second World War. The Festival of Britain was created as a celebration of British design and manufacturing. It therefore seemed only fitting that in 2008 the Southbank Centre approached Design-Nation and commissioned a series of works which would draw inspiration from the architecture of the centre whilst building bridges with a new generation of designers. Six designers took inspiration from the iconic architecture and history of the building through the production of desirable designs and products, which were manufactured and sold through retail sites at the centre.

One of the manufacturers who collaborated with the Eureka Project is Wentworth Pewter. Established in 1946, the company manufacture giftware and other articles in pewter and similar metals.

Richard Abdy of Wentworth Pewter explains how important it is that designers work in harmony with the manufacturer and not see that stage as a sterile necessity in the production of their works.

'One of the weaknesses a designer can have is not spending time in the factory and interacting with the people who will be making the pieces themselves. So much goodwill can be gained that helps throughout the process when people engage with one another.'

Richard explains that designers who are

sourcing manufacturers for small-scale batch production should 'listen to the crafts skill set within the factory and be prepared to be patient when explaining what is required. If necessary demonstrate that it can be achieved by doing it yourself, especially if you know something *can* be achieved.'

Rachel Moses encourages this communication between designer and manufacturer but highlights that although factory visits are important, 'It can be difficult for a supplier to make time for relatively small jobs, or even to make time to show you around the factory. It may be worth your while finding like-minded designers and to organise a group visit in the first instance. Be clear about who will market the product – you or the supplier?

'When forming relationships time is the only resource that you can't replace; propose weekly catch-up emails at the start of the relationship so that you can easily keep track of progress.'

'Design Nation seeks to add value to designers set up business by creating tailored business development opportunities. Its selected members have access to group stands at trade shows, selling exhibitions of silver , jewellery and giftware, informal meet and greet events and one-to-one 'Meet Design-Nation' networking sessions for those wanting to show existing work to retailers or perhaps work on a brief for a new product. All these opportunities are best described as self-help opportunities in that an introduction or meeting is arranged but it

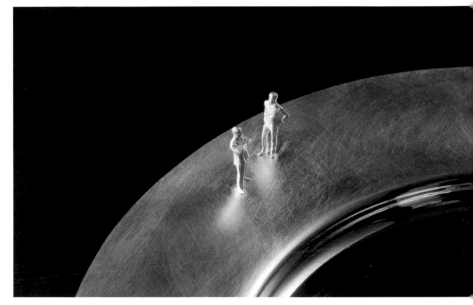

is up to the designer to capitalise on the situation'.

Rachel's final advice for designers wishing to manufacture work is 'Research your resources.' There are usually pockets of expertise in different parts of the country that can be identified through your local Business Link, seek advice from other designers creating work using a similar material or process. Contact government agencies in your area and visit tradeshows to identify possible suppliers.'

Design Nation offers a guide which may be purchased entitled *The Business Start-Up Guide for Designers and Makers*, which may be found at www.designnation.co.uk, while further organisations who offer invaluable support to designers may be found at the end of this book (see pp. 140–42).

Above
TITLE: People Plate
ARTIST: Rebecca Joselyn
MATERIAL: Sterling silver
DATE: 2007
PHOTO: Courtesy of the artist

One of the weaknesses a designer can have is not spending time in the factory and interacting with the people who will be making the pieces themselves.

Barbara Chandler is an unsung heroine of the design world. She currently writes a regular column on craft and design for the *Evening Standard*.

Barbara's eye for design and individuality has led to her pages in newspapers and magazines becoming a primary resource for retailers and design-conscious public alike. Her commitment to design and craft has linked these two fields together in the public mind, and her articles have often been about celebrating the person behind the object as much as the object itself. In addition to her journalism she is also an experienced photographer, has had many exhibitions including a selling one at Habitat and currently sells her prints through The Conran Shop.

Barbara started her career in journalism first on a local paper, and then on a trade magazine. She then moved to *Ideal Home* magazine, and became the furnishing editor. For several years, she had her own opinion section called Just Talking. She founded, wrote and took pictures for the *London Shopping Digest* for 20 years, visiting countless shops in London and the home counties, including many galleries and studios.

She became known as an advocate for good design, continuously seeking news for her readers on goods that scored highly on function, price and originality. She sought out the designers and manufacturers behind the products, and was one of the first journalists to champion the emerging trend of the designer-maker.

At the end of the 1980s, she was approached by the *London Evening Standard*. What started as a small column called Finishing Touches grew into regular double-page spreads. Then came *Homes & Property*, the Standard's regular home section, and Barbara became its design writer, as she still is today, now contributing a blog as well as being in print.

However, Barbara still feels that newspapers in general do not sufficiently value the excitement of news from the design, home-decoration and furnishing worlds. 'They will run reports from the Paris fashion shows as they happen, but in general are not interested in, for example, Milan.' Barbara has been able to change that attitude to some extent, and now contributes a regular report to the *Standard* on the Milan furniture fair and Maison & Objet in Paris.

Recently, Barbara became the design correspondent for *Homes & Gardens* magazine, and she chairs the judges for their Classic Design Award. In 2008, Barbara gained a special award for services to design from *The Designer* magazine. Indeed Barbara's career in journalism spans 35 years, and positions her as one of the country's most respected reporters within the design world.

Barbara initially started to write books. Most interesting was one entitled *Flat Broke*, perhaps an apt description for designer-makers. The book was aimed at people living in flats who were short of cash, for whom the solution was to make things. Barbara taught herself many skills including basic carpentry, knitting, macramé and crochet, which all helped to devise inspirational projects for her book. She raided skips, haunted charity shops and salvaged crates at a time when the word 'recycle' had not been invented. It was all part of the ethos of 1970s aesthetics.

Over the years, Barbara's columns have countless times brought the person behind the object to the foreground and told their stories, describing in detail not only what they make but how and why they do it. She is typically modest about her influence. 'From a journalist's perspective the aim is to promote these wonderful people that I have met, but it also comes from a quite specific need to fill my articles with exciting things. People often thank me for using their products in my pages, and when I get asked to present an award I say it is I who am thanking you for giving me wonderful material for my pages.'

Over the years, Barbara has seen the name for

her profession change from a 'home journalist' concerned with 'furnishing and decoration', to a 'design' writer covering 'interiors and lifestyle'. But basically she is still writing about the home, she says, and wonders whether the word design might sometimes alienate the core readership. Similarly 'designer-maker' is not a helpful description, she feels. 'What does it mean? Something different for everyone you talk to. It is a silly title. It sounds elitist, inaccessible and expensive.'

Gaining PR and press exposure is an important source of fuel for the career of any designer, craftsperson or maker. It is a primary shop window, where customers can see who you are and what your produce. Then they can seek out a stockist, armed with prior knowledge, and make an informed choice rather than a snap decision.

Barbara insists on the importance of a good story and not just a good image (although this is an important factor), and that for this reason any object should always be accompanied by a press release detailing the story behind its creation. 'I look upon the designer as a vital resource for my journalism. The person behind the piece is extremely important and could well be my story. You have to have a news value if you want things to go into the media. For this reason you need to be able to explian clearly what you are doing, what's new about it, why it is different and special, and above all, why people should buy it.'

Nowadays, even retailers are also incorporating the stories behind the work. Department stores are beginning to offer a point-of-sale display alongside the product with a sentence or two about how or where it was made. If you are a UK designer and a piece of yours is made in the UK or uses locally sourced materials, you should be shouting about it.

Barbara's hints and tips when sending work to the press are as follows:

'Do some homework first on exactly who to approach. Don't just send information to "the editor" and hope it will get there.

'Be conscious that journalists are constantly bombarded. Make sure your press release is concise and to the point.

'If emailing your image and release to the press, make sure you put the title and the subject matter in the email.

'Put your pictures in the main email Don't include them as attachments, as no one has time to open up attachments.

'Don't send someone a bulky letter – use postcards with your visuals on so that they cannot be missed. Make sure any CDs are clearly labelled.

'Make your communication different from the rest. Send an illustrated postcard for example, decorate the envelope or use handwriting.

'Never assume your discs will be opened – send them with thumbnails.

'Who, what, when and why are the first and main pieces of information needed in press releases.

'And finally, wait until you are absolutely ready to tell people about yourself – you only get one chance.'

They will run reports from the Paris shows as they happen, but try and flog them an idea from Milan and they don't want to know.

Sydney Levinson is a collector of craft, an ambassador for supporting British design talent, and a man with an eye for future trends and talents.

Sydney Levinson

ACCOUNTANT: ADDRESSING THE FEAR FACTOR

It just so happens that Sydney's day job is as a partner in a firm of chartered accountants in Doughty Street in London.

Through delivering practical workshops with organisations such as Design Nation and Cockpit Arts, where he offers advice for setting up in business as well as general accountancy help, Sydney has played an important role in helping young designers to meet their fears about accounts issues head-on.

In the early 1990s he joined the board of trustees at Cockpit Arts, which is an incubator for established, mid-career and start-up designers based across two sites in London. He continues to help in developing its programme and in creating opportunities for the 165 designers and makers housed within the organisation's studios.

For a creative person, to follow your dream and to have a goal is one thing, but to balance the books and apply a mathematical, business-minded approach is quite another.

One of the most fundamental lessons to learn for any young creative person to is to be prepared for what lies ahead. Having a good design is only the starting point. Selling, invoicing, tax, and sorting out your VAT returns can make or break your business.

Sydney's passion for helping others stems from his late father, who was an architect. However, in Sydney's eyes he was also a businessman, the longevity of whose practice owed as much to his entrepreneurship as to architectural skill. 'By running his practice as a business he made me understand the importance of instilling a sense of business into any creative enterprise. Over the years I have realised this need through my work with organisations such as the Crafts Council, The Prince's Trust, NESTA and as a visiting lecturer at higher-education institutions including the Royal College of Art.'

Most business start-ups are fresh out of university with little capital and little experience in accounts or how to source that crucial backing and funding opportunity. One of the most consistent areas of advice given by the designers selected in the book is to network.

When asked what advice he would offer to recent graduates and new designers wishing to embark on a creative career, Sydney replied, 'The most important advice I can give is to accept that creative talent alone is not enough to ensure survival and that time and respect must be given to business matters. Seek advice through recommendations from both your peers and your contemporaries. *The Business Start-Up Guide for Designers and Makers*, published by The Design Trust (now Design Nation), is an invaluable resource in this respect.

'The most important thing is to ensure that your market is properly tested before launching your business. Congratulatory plaudits at degree shows are not sufficient in this respect. You need to appreciate and allow for the investment of time needed to set up an infrastructure for your business, allocating equal importance to production, marketing, accounting and the protection of your own intellectual property. You will need to budget properly at the outset to ensure that you have sufficient funds to see you through this period either in terms of savings or some other parallel source of income.'

One of the most common areas where designers stumble is in pricing work. Universities rarely educate their graduates about the reality of the design world, although they have been getting better in recent years. It is true that most university students do not want to be torn away from workshops to sit through business studies, but such an attitude is perhaps not the best way to equip yourself for your future career. Also, having an understanding of the work of your contemporaries could be a practical solution for the future, as it enables you to see how your own designs fit into the wider marketplace. 'There is no golden rule for pricing work,' explains Sydney. 'You need to have a comprehensive understanding of your market both in terms of the customer and where your work will be sold. Your pricing must also be even – that is to say, work that you sell through shops and galleries should be the same price as that sold directly to the public through open studios or craft fairs.

A good accountant can be an asset to your business; a bad one a liability. Selecting the right one is therefore crucial. 'A good accountant should be able to add value to your business. The accountant should not merely be seen as a last-minute fix to fulfil statutory obligations but rather as a source of advice and experience prior to taking business decisions.'

Finding the time to do your accounts, organise your invoices and document expenses is hard enough, but designers and makers are often faced with a mountain to climb, which can be daunting and dull. When Sydney was asked for his top tip for overcoming this fear, he replied, 'In the words of Mary Poppins, "In every job that must be done there is an element of fun." Find the fun! It is essential to realise that the purpose of keeping accounts is not simply to meet statutory obligations but to help you understand your business and therefore to run it profitably and efficiently.'

 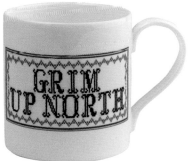 

You need to have a comprehensive understanding of your market both in terms of the customer and where your work will be sold. Your pricing must also be even – that is to say, work that you sell through shops and galleries should be the same price as that sold directly to the public through open studios or craft fairs.

Vessel

Selling work is obviously important to the life cycle of any craft and design business. Good ideas and beautifully finished items are the first steps on a road to success.

Having great ideas and beautifully crafted items is just the first part of the journey; the second is to ensure a successful route into the marketplace and, perhaps most importantly, to identify your audience.

One of the most visionary of all retail outlets is Vessel, a small gallery and retail shop situated in the heart of Notting Hill in London. Kensington Park Road is a leafy street in one of the capital's most fashionable neighbourhoods, home to a number of independent retailers all thriving on the demographics of the area. Artists, musicians and writers all flock here to set up their homes and studios. With this comes an uncompromising spending power and the need to have the next name in design or the most sought-after name in craft and production. The best of craft skill and small-scale batch production is often showcased at Vessel.

The gallery prides itself on changing exhibitions which tell stories, creating a link to the potential buyer and putting the maker behind the work on the same platform as the pieces themselves. Bringing knowledge to the buyer and creating a relationship between the maker and the buyer is key to Vessel's mission; to simply offer a piece of craft to take away is not enough for Nadia Demetriou Ladas, the owner of Vessel, and Art Director Angel Monzon. It's about the story, the materials and the process behind the object as much as it is about the appearance of a vessel.

Established by Nadia in the spring of 1999, Vessel has showcased some of the most exciting names on the designer-maker scene, as well as some of the most visionary designers within product design and art. They marry successfully the idea of a niche boutique and a gallery experience, which department stores and other retailers can only aspire to.

As the gallery's website puts it, 'Everything in the shop has been chosen with passion, and it's a pas-sion I hope to share with all my customers. That rush of excitement when you see something awe-inspiring. All the objects at Vessel fall into Walter Gropius's definition of good design, that they should have beauty, quality, function and affordability.'

What is evident in the success of the gallery-cum-retail space is the meticulous selection process which Nadia and Angel jointly undertake to ensure Vessel retains that passion. They visit countless trade fairs and exhibitions in both the UK and Europe, often sourcing the next trends and fashions within interiors but most importantly encouraging continued growth of the hands-on skill and craftsmanship behind the creation of these products.

Vessel has reinvented the shopping experience for purchasing craft and design. They realised from the outset the importance of creating a destination where the visitor can engage with the work. To this end, even window displays are often created by guest visual merchandisers to tell the story from outside the shop of what one may find within.

When I asked Nadia how designers and crafts-people should approach retailers, her reply was, 'Well, the first and most surprisingly forgotten thing is to do some proper research. There's no point applying to totally the wrong kind of gallery – it's a waste of your time, effort and money. Study the market and really find the right gallery to apply to – don't just have a scattergun approach. Personalise the letter or email as much as possible. For example, find out who the owner is and get their name spelt correctly – that way, at least you'll be sure you are reaching the right person.

'Certainly the most important thing is to have good images of your work – one stunning shot is much more effective than a thousand jumbled words. You shouldn't be aiming to send a thesis on your artistic philosophy, just a clear, short statement

Below

TITLE: Maze, side view.
ARTIST: Anu Penttinen
DATE: 2009

MATERIAL: Fused and
kiln-formed glass

summarising what your work is about, how it is made, what materials are used and giving an indication of the retail price. Three or four sentences really are enough. Negotiating a wholesale price is a delicate art and can be tackled later once there has been an initial positive response, but showing that you are already aware of commercial realities bodes well for any future collaboration.

'You could then offer to fix an appointment to come to the gallery and show some samples. The most annoying thing is when people simply show up and demand to be seen at what may be an inconvenient time, especially if the work isn't suitable in the first place.

'Finally, a good tactic (which needs to be used skilfully) is perhaps to mention some other galleries or competitors that you are "in discussions" with There is nothing like a bit of rivalry to spur people into action!'

'Selling work through retailers can be difficult, and there is an element of "We like to find you" rather than "You come to us" in the philosophy of many retail owners. Most importantly, when contacting a retailer you need to remember that their time is precious, so you're not guaranteed a response.

'Being prepared is essential, as first impressions really do count.'

Certainly the most important thing is to have good images of your work – one stunning shot is much more effective than a thousand jumbled words.

Ian Rudge is an event organiser and was co-founder of the 100% Design exhibition, which over the past decade has become renowned as the UK's leading contemporary interiors event.

Ian started 100% Design to meet a need he identified for a contemporary design show in the UK, and it now attracts the contract market, key manufacturers and star designers. Ian knew a number of designer-makers within his social circle, and realised that there was a lack of places to exhibit British design and that there was also an increase in people wanting to view and buy original design-led products. In addition the show was intended to provide a commercial platform where designers could meet with larger sectors of the design community including retailers, architects and specifiers (a term given to people in charge of interior projects or site-specific commissions).

The exhibition was backed by a well-written research and development plan, drawn up by someone who clearly listens to his audience. Rudge works with designers and makers and asks them which clients they wish to attract and where they wish to attract them from, and he sees it as a mission to try and put this jigsaw of supply and demand together.

Ian sold 100% Design to Reed Exhibitions in 2000 but remained committed to the show as the event organiser, and in 2007 started a new design exhibition called Tent London.

The idea of Ian and his business partner Jimmy MacDonald, the duo feel Tent is based on further intuitive thinking in favour of the designer-maker,

and the format allows room for experimentation.

There are a number of different areas within Tent London, the aim being to attract a wide selection of mutually sympathetic design practices. As with 100% Design there is still a leaning towards supporting new talent, and to this end Tent offers the Talent Zone, which, in the same vein as One Year On at the New Designers Exhibition and 100% Design Futures, features work by recent graduates.

In addition to this, Tent also includes areas where you can buy vintage design, as well as areas that promote up-and-coming designers and established companies. There are also 'blank canvas' spaces where the designer can create entire environments and let their creative imaginations run free.

Ian Rudge's top tips for designers exhibiting work are, in short, 'preparation, pricing, exhibiting, promotion'. At greater length, he says, 'Have a resolved design and make sure you know what it is costing to make. Price the product at a wholesale price, and identify your intended purchasers.

'Select the right exhibition for you. Exhibitions work very well but you have to ensure that they are accompanied with press and promotion. Make sure you have the right information at the show and enough information packs and leaflets at the start of the show to last you.

'Prepare a website so that any potential purchasers can view it at their leisure away from the

Have a resolved design and make sure you know what it is costing to make. Price the product at a wholesale price, and identify your intended purchasers.

show. A lot of people make the mistake of exhibiting but not having a plan of action on how to follow up.

'Be prepared to answer questions such as what is the delivery time, what are the payment options and who else is selling it.

'Remember that people are visual buyers and a space should be well-considered and appealing – not overpowering but neat and professional.

'Do not put too many things on the stand, and use repetition of product to show the visitor what it is that you make.

'Use plain bookcases and do not confuse the visitor about what it is that you make.

'Use labels to let people know items are for sale.

'People often forget the importance of lighting, so do consider how the product will be lit.

'And finally, remember to tap into all the services the exhibition has to offer, especially if this is the first show you have done. Many shows offer a training-day event, or there may be advice in exhibition manuals. Never be afraid to ask the show organisers for help – it's what they are there for.'

Below
TITLE: Arc Chair
ARTIST: Tom Raffield
MATERIAL: English Oak
DATE: 2008
PHOTO: Mark Wallcock

Be prepared to answer questions such as what is the delivery time, what are the payment options and who else is selling it.

Thorsten van Elten is a retailer and distributor/manufacturer. He spotted a niche in the market, feeling that there was no one in the UK giving support to the designer-maker ready to find manufacturers.

His success has come from assisting designers who have created, and in many cases started producing, the product themselves, but require assistance to further their business and in distributing their wares.

Thorsten started his business in 2002, after having worked for SCP for five years in various areas such as wholesale, export, buying and merchandising. SCP is a shop set up by Sheridan Coakley in 1985 to sell classic furniture designs of the Modern Movement whilst also aiming to manufacture new products.

This experience offered Thorsten the opportunity to gain a complete overview and an all-round education in how to run a successful business, giving him the appetite for starting his own company. 'I loved the whole ethos behind it,' he says of his time at SCP, but also admits that there came a time to strike out on his own. 'I wanted to do this for myself. There is only so much you can do by working for another company. It felt like the natural progression.'

Thorsten spotted a niche in the market, feeling that there was no one in the UK giving support to the designer-maker ready to find manufacturers to forward their ideas and turn them into commercial designs.

Creating a platform containing numerous different products benefited both his business and the larger retailers and department stores. They found that they could get various objects from a single supplier that would suit different departments within their stores, making it worth their while setting up an account with Thorsten's business.

From the outset, Thorsten began his search looking for products he would want to have made himself. His first find was Ed Carpenter's Pigeon Light, which he discovered while working for SCP. Then in 2002 he launched his business at 100% Design with the Pigeon Light and six other prod-

ucts. Retailers then came to Thorsten and bought products off him as a supplier.

Thorsten is keen that the products he offers should be stamped with the individuality of their makers. 'It is important that the designer's name is still attached to the product. It's a product that they have made and their personality is part of it. I am just looking after it for them!'

When asked what he looks for in a designer before agreeing to represent the product, he replied, 'It's usually instinct. Most often it's a no if I don't love it straightaway.'

Thorsten does not design any of the products he sells. He knows that his strengths lie in guiding the designer-maker along the correct route and inputting into the design where needed. His team work closely alongside the designer-maker throughout the journey from initial concept to manufactured product.

In 2004 Thorsten opened his first retail outlet, Thorsten van Elten, in Warren Street in London, offering for the first time a stable environment in which to showcase the work. Though the shop is no longer there, he is very pleased to have made that move. 'This shop worked phenomenally well in bringing across to people my ethos and my ideas.'

Press for Thorsten 'is like a double-edged sword. Sometimes if you get a lot of publicity people get the wrong impression that you must be doing fantastically well because they see your product everywhere, and then potentially they could get bored of it from seeing it across so many magazines. Often the reality is that only a dozen have been sold. It's the perception people have of you.'

Thorsten's advice for the next generation of designers who want to enter the marketplace is as follows:

'Figure out and be realistic about where you want to be and what you want to do. Do you want to build up a business or build up your name as a designer?

'Only by researching, visiting select shows, being inspired and finding your own direction can this picture be built upon and grown. New Designers is a great platform for the launch of any new designer. A question to be asked is whether art colleges and universities are helping graduates with this and preparing them for the outside design world.

'There are two ways to go after leaving education. You either go out and work for somebody and earn money, or you do it by yourself and don't earn money! You do it for the love.

'Designer-makers need to know what they want to do and where their work is placed. There is nothing worse than receiving work where the designer hasn't researched its audience.

'Don't look too much into today's design world, but instead create original ideas and concepts. Everyone needs inspiration, but if you take it too much from now, people will pick up on it and see you as not forward-thinking enough. Originality always prevails.'

Below
TITLE: Labware Lamps
ARTIST: Benjamin Hubert
MATERIAL: Blown Glass
DATE: 2008
PHOTO: Star
Photographers

Where's Hot To Shop?

THE INSIDER'S GUIDE TO BUYING OR SEEING CRAFT AND DESIGN

This section details the places and spaces you can go to buy, view, visit and indulge yourself in the world of craft, design and product. Compiled with the designers and makers themselves, this guide offers you an insider's knowledge of the best boutiques, gracious galleries and exhilarating exhibitions which will leave you inspired, while giving you the chance to buy conversation pieces for homes and interiors.

TOP SHOPS
Batch designers' top UK retailers with their finger on the crafts and design pulse.

Beyond the Valley
2 Newburgh Street
London
W1F 7RD
+44 (0)20 7437 7338

Caravan
3 Redchurch Street
London
E2 7DJ
+44 (0)20 7033 3532

Concrete Wardrobe
50a Broughton Street
Edinburgh
EH1 3SA
+44 (0)131 558 7130

The Conran Shop Fulham
Michelin House
81 Fulham Road
London
SW3 6RD
+44 (0)20 7589 7401

The Conran Shop Marylebone
55 Marylebone High Street
London

W1U 5HS
+44 (0)20 7723 2223

Designers Guild, London
267–77 Kings Road
London
SW3 5EN
+44 (0)20 7351 5775

Heal's
Stores in London, Brighton, Kingston,
Manchester, Guildford, West Yorkshire.
+44 (0)8700 240 780

Liberty
Great Marlborough Street
London
W1B 5AH
+44 (0)20 7734 1234

Lifestyle Bazaar
11a Kingsland Road
Shoreditch
London
E2 8AA
+44 (0)20 739 9427

Lucas Bond
45 Bedford Hill
London
SW12 9EY
+44 (0)20 8675 9300

Mint
2 North Terrace
Alexander Square
London
SW3 2BA
+44 (0)20 7225 2228

SCP
135–139 Curtain Road
London
EC2A 3BX
+44 (0)20 77391869

Shelf
40 Cheshire Street
London
E2 6EH
+44 (0)20 7739 9444

Southbank Centre Gallery Shop
Royal Festival Hall
Festival Terrace
London
+44 (0)20 7921 0771

Vessel
114 Kensington Park Road
London
W11 2PW
+44 (0)20 727 8001

Victoria and Albert Museum Shop
V&A South Kensington
Cromwell Road
London
SW7 2RL
+44 (0)20 7942 2000

Yorkshire Sculpture Park (YSP) Shop
Bretton Hall, Bretton
Wakefield
WF4 4LG
+44 (0)1924 832631

The designers' top international retailers

The Collection, France
33 rue de Poitou
75003 Paris
France
+33 (0) 1 42 77 04 20

De La Espada Store
33 Greene Street
New York
USA
NY 10013
+1 212 625 1039

Design Forum Helsinki
Erottajankatu 7
00120 Helsinki
Finland
+358 9 622 0810

Droog Design Store
Staalstraat 7a/b
1011 JJ Amsterdam
Netherlands
+31 (0)20 523 5050

Home Autour du Monde France
8 rue des Francs Bourgeois
75003 Paris
France
+33 (0)1 42 77 06 08

Living Motif
5-17-1 Roppnong
Minato-ku
Tokyo
Japan
+81 3 3587 2784

Museum of Modern Art Design Store (MOMA) USA
44 West 53rd Street
New York
NY 10019
USA
+1 212 767 1050

Star Provisions USA
1198 Howell Mill Road
Atlanta
GA 30318
+1 404 365 0410

GALLERIES AND EXHIBITIONS UK
The designers' top galleries for showcasing the cream of design and craft talent and for exhibitions featuring cutting-edge design and craft.

Carpenters Workshop Gallery
3 Albemarle Street
London
W1S 4HE
+44 (0)20 3051 5939

Contemporary Applied Arts (CAA)
2 Percy Street
London
W1T 1DD
+44 (0)207 436 2344

Dazzle (touring exhibition)
Mainly for jewellery.
Edinburgh, Glasgow, Manchester, London
www.dazzle-exhibitions.com

Goldsmiths' Fair, London
www.thegoldsmiths.co.uk/events
for details on locations for each exhibition.

The Harley Gallery
Welbeck
Worksop
Nottinghamshire
S80 3LW
+44 (0)1909 501700

Hub
National Centre for Craft and Design
Carre Street
Sleaford
Lincolnshire
+44 (0)1529 308710

Lustre (annual exhibition)
Lakeside Arts Centre
University of Nottingham
Nottingham
NG7 2RD
+44 (0)115 846 7777

Origin & Collect (both annual exhibitions)
www.craftscouncil.org for details on locations for each exhibition.

Ruthin Craft Centre
Park Road
Ruthin
Denbighshire
LL15 1BB
+44 (0)1824 704774

Scottish Gallery
16 Dundas Street
Edinburgh
EH3 6HZ
+44 (0)131 558 1200

WHERE TO SHOP ON THE WORLD WIDE WEB.
The top virtual destinations as selected by the designers and makers.
www.aplusrstore.com
www.bouf.com
www.branchhome.com
www.charlesandmarie.com
www.designedinengland.com
www.hiddenart.com
www.notonthehighstreet.com
www.pedlars.com
www.supermarkethq.com
www.thorstenvanelten.com

Helpful Addresses and Contacts

100% Design
www.100percentdesign.co.uk
100% Design is now a worldwide brand in cities including Tokyo and Shanghai. 100% Design forms part of the London Festival.

ACID (Anti Copying in Design)
+44 (0)845 644 3617
www.acid.uk.com
An international organisation that actively supports its members in combating copyright infringement. It has a large membership base drawn from creative businesses in every area of the design industry.

Arts Council England
+44 (0)845 300 6200
www.artscouncil.org.uk
Provides grants for the arts, administering funds of up to £30,000 to a range of artists, designers and makers, from individual one-off projects to organisations. Application packs are on the website.

BJGF
The British Jewellery, Giftware & Finishing Federation
+44 (0)121 236 2657
www.bjgf.org
The Federation represents trade associations with creative companies in Britain.

British Jewellers' Association (BJA)
www.bja.org.uk
The British Jewellers' Association is a national trade association that promotes and protects the growth and prosperity of UK jewellery and silverware suppliers.

BEDG
British European Design Group
+44 (0)20 8940 7857
www.bedg.org
The British European Design Group has been a key force in the promotion of the UK creative industries in the United Kingdom, Continental and Eastern Europe, North and South America, the Middle East, Hong Kong and the People's Republic of China.

Business Link
+44 (0)845 600 9006
www.businesslink.gov.uk
National business advice service supported by the British Government with a network of local branches. A free business advice and support service offering impartial advice to small companies of all kinds including business start-ups, mid-career and established practices. A number of grants are offered to cover various needs including development and research.

Cockpit Arts
+44 (0)207 419 1959
www.cockpitarts.com
The largest provider in London of one-to-one support, seminars and workshops for designer-makers at any level of career. Programmes they offer include Developing Professional Practice and the Designer-Maker in Action.

Craft Central
+44 (0)207 251 0276
www.craftcentral.org.uk
Offers studio spaces for crafts-people and runs Craft Central Network, a support mechanism for makers. Organisers of the Reflect Forward award scheme, which gives makers a chance to unveil cutting-edge, contemporary work, and also the Bright Ideas scheme, which supports the development of new products.

Crafts Council
+44 (0)207 806 2500
www.craftscouncil.org.uk
The national organisation for contemporary crafts in England and Wales. The Crafts Council controls a number of awards. The Crafts Council 'Collective' is a new programme for designers and makers to develop individual career paths including network opportunities, business growth and start up support. In addition the council have added the new Hot House scheme for emerging makers.

Craftspace
+44 (0)121 608 6668
www.craftspace.co.uk
A craft development organisation which offers a range of advisory services in the arts as well as creating a programme of touring exhibitions and collaborations.

Design Boom
www.designboom.com
Host of a group exhibition stand of international design professionals from around the world at the ICFF exhibition.

Design Council
+44 (0)207 420 5200
www.designcouncil.org.uk
The Design Council 'believe design can help people to do what they do, better.' Funded by the UK government to promote the use of design throughout the UK's businesses and public services.

Design Factory
+44 (0)1529 414830
www.designfactory.org.uk
The Design Factory offers business development and support for the designer-maker by raising profiles and creating opportunities for the successful growth of creative businesses. Acts as a voice for high-quality and innovative design and craft industries.

Design Nation
+44 (0)20 7320 2895
www.designnation.co.uk
Formerly the Design Trust, it offers support and business guidance for designers, makers and students as well as promoting British Design through its website, catalogue and networking opportunities. Membership also offers access to bursary schemes at exhibitions and trade fairs

Enterprise Centre for the Creative Arts (ECCA)
www.ecca-london.org
Available to graduates of the University of the Arts London who have set up their own practices in the last three years or are planning to start one. It gives support and advice for artists on tax and accounting, as well as offering free seminars, one-to-one business advice and workshops.

Hidden Art
+44 (0)20 7729 3800/3301
www.hiddenart.com
Dedicated to promoting and supporting designer-makers and creating direct access for all to new designs.

Highlands and Islands Enterprise
+44 (0)1463 234171
www.hie.co.uk
The Scottish Government's economic and community development agency for a diverse region covering more than half of Scotland.

Design Gap
+44 (0)121 242 0242
www.designgap.co.uk
Assist in the promotion of high quality, innovative, contemporary UK artist-makers and designer-producers

MARK
+44 (0)1326 375514
www.markproduct.com
Championing the skilled craftsmanship of local manufacturing whilst reflecting the values of contemporary Cornwall.

Metropolitan Works
+44 (0)207 320 1827
www.metropolitanworks.org
A support centre for creative industries in London, helping designers and manufacturers transfer new ideas to the marketplace. Provides workshops and courses, advice and exhibitions.

Nesta
+44 (0)207 438 2500
www.nesta.org.uk
Grants offered to creative graduates who need help in setting up their own businesses, such as the Creative Pioneer and the Insight Out initiative.

New Designers (One Year On)
+44 (0)20 7288 6453
www.newdesigners.com
One Year On is a satellite event

run as part of New Designers. It specifically presents approximately 50 designer-makers who are within one year of graduating or within one year of being in business.

The P&O Makower Trust (Penelope and Oliver Makower)
www.bishopsland.org.uk
Concerned with the promotion and exhibition of contemporary silver and the support of young silversmiths.

The Prince's Trust
+44 (0)207 543 1234
www.princes-trust.org.uk
Offers grants and training to help those between 18 and 30 set up their own business. Also includes provision of low-interest loans and education grants.

The Queen Elizabeth Scholarship Trust
+44 (0)207 828 2268
www.qest.org.uk
Offers awards to finance further training, study and practical experiences for those craftspeople who want to improve on the trade and craft skills they already have.

Red Dot Design Award
www.red-dot.de
Manufacturers and designers of a wide variety of industrial products can enter their work all year round in different product groups for the coveted Red Dot Award.

Rotterdam Design Prize
www.designprijs.nl
The Rotterdam Design Prize is a national prize open to all design disciplines. The award of 15,000 euros is presented every two years. Any designer, studio or company based in the Netherlands may enter.

Shell Livewire

+44 (0)191 423 6229
www.shell-livewire.org
Aimed at the 16-to-30 age group,
this support network provides practical advice in starting up your
own business.

Society of Designer Craftsmen

+44 (0)207 739 3663
www.societyofdesignercraftsmen.
org.uk
Membership organisation for the
designer-maker.

Tent London

+44 (0)20 7739 5561
www.tentlondon.co.uk
The Tent London design event
showcases a vibrant mix of
contemporary design and vintage
design. The trade and public
exhibition takes place in central
London and celebrates new talent,
product design and digital media.

The Goldsmiths' Company

+44 (0)20 7606 7010
www.thegoldsmiths.co.uk
Offers support for craft and industry.

UK Trade and Investment

+44 (0)20 7215 8000
www.uktradeinvest.gov.uk
Offers invaluable support for
exhibiting work overseas, and
also business advice.

Wingate Scholarships

www.wingatescholarships.org.uk
Offers scholarships for pioneering
original works of intellectual, scientific, artistic or environmental value.

Above

TITLE: Goldfish Light
ARTIST: Scabetti
MATERIAL: 186 Bone china fish with
24 carat gold lustre
DATE: 2009

Contributing Artists' Contacts

Index

CERAMICS

Andrew Tanner
www.andrewtannerdesign.co.uk
Bodo Sperlein
www.bodosperlein.com
KleinReid
www.kleinreid.com
Nicola Malkin
www.nicolamalkin.com
Anja Lubach
www.anjalubach.com
Kathleen Hills
www.kathleenhills.co.uk
Qubus Studio
www.qubus.cz
Scabetti
www.scabetti.co.uk

FURNITURE

Eiry Rock
www.eiryrock.co.uk
Marina Bautier
www.lamaisondemarina.com
Pottinger & Cole
www.pottingerandcole.co.uk
Gareth Neal
www.garethneal.co.uk
Paul Loebach
www.paulloebach.com
Tom Raffield
www.tomraffield.com

GLASS

Anu Penttinen
www.nounoudesign.fi
Kathryn Wightman
www.kathrynwightmanglass.co.uk
Stuart Akroyd
www.stuartakroydglass.com
Heather Gillespie
www.gillespieglass.co.uk
Rothschild & Bickers
www.rothschildbickers.com
Simon Moore
www.simonmoore.uk.com

MULTIDISCIPLINARY

Alissia Melka-Teichroew
www.byamt.com
Benjamin Hubert
www.benjaminhubert.co.uk
Design Glut
www.designglut.com

Molo
www.molodesign.com
Autoban
www.autoban212.com
Chris Kabel
www.chriskabel.com
Michael Marriott
www.michaelmarriott.com

TEXTILES

Anne Kyyrö Quinn
www.annekyyroquinn.com
Etcetera Media
www.etceteramedia.com
Margo Selby
www.margoselby.com
Ingrid Tait
www.taitandstyle.co.uk
Donna Wilson
www.donnawilson.com
Helen Amy Murray
www.helenamymurray.com
Stella Corall www.stellacorrall.co.uk

Teresa Green
www.teresagreen.co.uk

METAL AND JEWELLERY

Anne Christensen
www.anechristensen.com
Jane Adam
www.janeadam.com
Sidsel Dorph-Jensen
www.dorphjensen.com
Angela Cork
www.angelacork.co.uk
Rebecca Joselyn
www.designsinsilver.co.uk

SURFACE DESIGN AND DECORATION

Deborah Bowness
www.deborahbowness.com
Ilias Fotopoulos
www.ilias.com.au
Tracy Kendall
www.tracykendall.com
Ella Doran
www.elladoran.co.uk
Lizzie Allen
www.lizzieallen.co.uk